MOSQUITO NIGHT INTRUDER ACE

The Intruder Pilot

They have a job which demands brilliance at everything, together with very special eyesight, they make up only 6 per cent of RAF pilots. We make what we call super-pilots and would be star turns either at flying bombers or fighters. Of these, a proportion only have what we call suitable dark adaption, this means that they don't suffer from night blindness, have no inclination to be upset by sudden flashes of light.

All night fighters need to possess a rapid recovery curve and to be able to put up a constant performance. Patience, dash, and top-notch flying in view of the speed in which they have to land their aircraft at night are also necessary. They should, in fact, be super-pilots!

Unnamed RAF Medical Professor

MOSQUITO NIGHT INTRUDER ACE

Group Captain Bertie Rex O'Bryen Hoare
DSO & Bar, DFC & Bar

DANNY BURT

AIR WORLD

AIR WORLD

MOSQUITO NIGHT INTRUDER ACE
Group Captain Bertie Rex O'Bryen Hoare DSO & Bar, DFC & Bar

First published in Great Britain in 2023 by
Air World
An imprint of
Pen & Sword Books Ltd
Yorkshire – Philadelphia

ISBN 978 1 39901 786 2

Typeset by SJmagic DESIGN SERVICES, India.

Printed and bound in the UK by CPI Group (UK) Ltd.

Pen & Sword Books Limited incorporates the imprints of Atlas, Archaeology, Aviation, Discovery, Family History, Fiction, History, Maritime, Military, Military Classics, Politics, Select, Transport, True Crime, Air World, Frontline Publishing, Leo Cooper, Remember When, Seaforth Publishing, The Praetorian Press, Wharncliffe Local History, Wharncliffe Transport, Wharncliffe True Crime and White Owl.

For a complete list of Pen & Sword titles please contact

PEN & SWORD BOOKS LIMITED
47 Church Street, Barnsley, South Yorkshire, S70 2AS, England
E-mail: enquiries@pen-and-sword.co.uk
Website: www.pen-and-sword.co.uk

Or
PEN AND SWORD BOOKS
1950 Lawrence Rd, Havertown, PA 19083, USA
E-mail: Uspen-and-sword@casematepublishers.com
Website: www.penandswordbooks.com

CONTENTS

Foreword   vii

Preface   ix

Acknowledgements   x

Author's Comments   xii

Early Life   1

Commissioned into the Royal Air Force   8
    1936   8

A Professional Flying Club   13
    1937–40   13

Nelson of the RAF   20

Flight Commander 23 Squadron   29
    1941   29

Officer Commanding 23 Squadron   46
    1942   46

Commanding Officer 23 Squadron   51

60 Operational Training Unit   65
    1943   65

Commanding Officer 605 Squadron   75
    1944   89

Station Commander RAF Little Snoring   110
    1945   135

Bertie's and Lucy's Wedding   142

The Loss of an Ace   148
  1946–47   148

Personal Reflections of Wing Commander Bertie Hoare   177
  A Beautiful Aeroplane   177

  Halifax NA259   179

  Posted out the Squadron with a DFC   180

  The Officers Mess Garden   186

Annexes   191
  Operational Flying Record Log   191

  Combat Claims   196

  Physical Training in Blackout Conditions   198

  Lorenz Visual System   203

  Report on G.A.F Night Fighting from the Interrogation of Prisoners 204

Abbreviations   226

Index   230

FOREWORD

Air Commodore R.S. (Rick) Peacock-Edwards
CBE AFC FRAeS FCIM

I feel deeply privileged and honoured to have been asked to write this Foreword for *Mosquito Night Intruder Ace* by the author, Danny Burt, himself a great enthusiast for life, and a bundle of energy and ideas. I commend Danny, from the outset, for writing this book and telling the fascinating story of Group Captain 'Bertie' Hoare, a true hero from World War Two. However, there are other reasons why I am so delighted to carry out this task. My own father was a World War Two Battle of Britain Hurricane pilot who started his RAF career flying the Fairey Battle with No 150 Squadron. He was based in France from September 1939 to June 1940 when the squadron was evacuated back to the mainland UK. I note that Bertie Hoare started his flying career also flying the Fairey Battle before going on to fly, with distinction, the Blenheim, Havoc, Boston and, finally, the Mosquito. My second reason is because one of my good friends, Colin Bell, now in his 102nd year and still very active, was himself an acclaimed Mosquito pilot who flew fifty missions over Germany, thirteen of them over Berlin. The Mosquito, on which Bertie achieved so much, was a very special aircraft, and I am delighted that one is currently being restored to full flying condition in the south of England.

This is a story that I am so pleased has now been told because the subject of the book, 'Bertie' Hoare, deserves to be remembered for his wartime exploits, for his leadership qualities, for his exceptional ability as a pilot and, especially, as a night fighter 'Intruder' pilot. Indeed, he was undoubtedly one of the great night fighter pilots. The award of two DFCs, two DSOs and no fewer than three Mentioned in Dispatches are testament to the achievements and courage of Bertie. The fact that he flew over 100 combat missions in the night 'intruder' role with the sight of only one eye (he lost the use of one eye early in his flying career), makes the achievement that much more amazing and, to me, puts him in the same league as Douglas Bader for achievement against adversity.

The author was inspired to write this book when he visited the airfield at Little Snoring, previously RAF Little Snoring during World War Two, and where Bertie had been the station commander. His meeting with the current airfield owner, Tommy Cushing, himself passionate about the history of the airfield, and his subsequent discussions, and a visit to St Andrew's Church, itself very relevant to the story, have all played a key part in the telling of this story. To say that I enjoyed reading the story is an understatement, I found it so compelling that I simply wanted to learn more, I could not stop reading.

You will enjoy reading this book which does justice to a true hero, and a great character. The fact that 'Bertie' Hoare was the proud owner of a 6-inch-wide handlebar moustache, itself such a characteristic of the RAF flying hero, implies that he was both a man of substance and great character. There is no truer statement.

Rick Peacock-Edwards
February 2022

PREFACE

The Royal Air Force is immersed in military history and abundantly rich with heroes. Their daring acts of valour are etched with pride in the hearts and souls of the British nation. Famous RAF pilot names such as Douglas Bader, 'Sailor' Malan, and Bob Stanford Tuck, with many others have fired the imagination and inspired many of our sons and daughters of today.

This book documents the true life adventures of perhaps a less well known, but equally courageous combat pilot of the Second World War: Group Captain Bertie Hoare, RAF, also known to his friends and family as 'Sammy' or 'Rex'. This book is an account of a gallant and very brave man indeed! It explores the extraordinary life of an early exponent in the development of Royal Air Force night Intruder tactics, having lost the sight in one eye early in his military career but miraculously still able to accomplish over 100 combat operations. It concludes with the love for his wife Lucy, and the tragic loss of his life at the incredibly young age of 34 in a post-war flying-accident.

ACKNOWLEDGEMENTS

This book has been a pleasure to write; its outcome has only been made possible by the assistance and encouragement provided to me by the various people and departments who have gone out of their way to help answer the many questions I have asked.

First, my daughter Freya; I owe her my sincere love and thanks. Second, I am indebted to Tommy Cushing, the owner of Little Snoring airfield, this once busy Intruder base named Royal Air Force Little Snoring. Listening to his personal accounts on how he had met this Intruder ace in person during the Second World War is truly remarkable.

Bertie's immediate family, Rosy, Sam, Lexy and Gordon, and close family friend, Elizabeth. I am indebted to them all for all their personal support and for sharing their emotions and memories, without these personal reflections I would not have been able to write this book.

George Stewart, a Royal Canadian Air Force Mosquito pilot, himself a combat ace, having served with Bertie. I must thank him for his own personal reflections. Andy Thomas, and Martin Bowman who have provided great levels of research and information, enough to write their own history on this specific personality. For the other 'team', Chris Goss, for his exceptional knowledge and information detailing Luftwaffe combat engagements.

Invaluable help was granted from The National Archives, Kew. Wing Commander Erica Ferguson, RAF, and all members of the Air Historical Branch. Sharon, at the RAF Museum, Hendon, for answering and helping with my research questions via email and post. All applicable RAF squadrons and their respective associations for providing a great depth of detail and information from an extensive library and network of paperwork and records.

ACKNOWLEDGEMENTS

My publishing team, Amy Jordan and Martin Mace, who have spent endless hours putting my complicated notes into some structure, so it forms the basis of this book. Many others have provided me with useful information; hopefully, I have acknowledged their help by direct reference in their appropriate summary. Thus, for any omissions on my part, I hereby humbly apologise.

AUTHOR'S COMMENTS

'In Memory of Lucy Hoare, who I promised I would write this book for'

On a sunny afternoon in early May 2020, I was looking for an area of land in Norfolk to conduct some military training with UK Royal Air Force FGR4 Typhoon aircraft. It needed to provide good clear airspace, and quiet enough to ward off any unwanted visitors. This was to assist with training and rehearsal of close air support procedures, this being my core job for many years and from where my passion for RAF history originated. My finger landed on the map at a disused wartime airfield, oddly named Little Snoring, Norfolk. I jumped in my work truck and drove the two hours from my home base in Lincolnshire to the beautiful setting of Little Snoring village. On arrival I found the disused airfield and noticed at the end of the abandoned runway a beautiful quaint church, deciding to go and have a 'mooch' around and see if there was any connection to the once busy life at RAF Little Snoring. The eighteenth century St Andrews church is situated in a tranquil setting, and I was excited to find information inside the small church displaying the many victories the RAF Mosquito squadrons had claimed when based at the airfield when it was operational, hand painted, on three large wooden panels. These once resided on the wall of the station officers' mess before successfully being rescued and brought to the church by Mrs Bessie Whitehead, a local lady who had a strong connection with the airfield, before the building was demolished.

I continued my adventure through the church cemetery and noticed a single military style shaped headstone in the corner, beautifully shaded under a lone tree. Positioned in a way that it looked over the now deserted runway. I walked over to view the name and details on the headstone. I was surprised to see the details of a female senior WAAF officer, Lucy

Hoare. I noticed that the inscription in addition mentioned the loss of her late husband, Group Captain B.R.O'B. Hoare, RAF, whose name is commemorated at the Kranji cemetery, Singapore. The headstone recorded that he was the Station Commander here, at RAF Little Snoring, during the latter part of the Second World War.

After visiting Lucy's grave, I had the pleasure of meeting the present airfield landowner, Mr Tommy Cushing; his knowledge on the history of the airfield and the exploits of its wartime service was remarkable. Soon he was reciting the story of an RAF pilot with an extremely long handlebar moustache who had shown him around a Mosquito aircraft when he was just 8 years old. Here, my quest started in earnest, and I soon found out that the pilot Tommy was talking about was actually Bertie Hoare. The name inscribed on Lucy's headstone boasted an extraordinary, famous military career as an RAF combat pilot and night Intruder ace during the Second World War. As a military researcher I was amazed that the history of this RAF pilot had never been comprehensively documented in any detail. So, after much deliberation, I decided to take on the privileged invitation to write his history. It has been a challenge but also extremely rewarding, and I hope the reader enjoys this small book on an exceptionally large character!

Danny Burt

Left: Lucy's headstone at St Andrews Church, Little Snoring. She wanted to be buried close to the airfield where she met Bertie, her husband; she would always comment that this is where she was at her happiest. He held the rank of Acting Group Captain when Station Commander of RAF Little Snoring. (Author's collection)

Below: St Andrews Church, Little Snoring; believed to be dated pre-Norman, possibly Saxon, also mentioned in the Domesday book. As Station Commander at RAF Little Snoring, Bertie decided to restore the church and hold a service every Sunday, during wartime years the congregation was always higher. (Author's collection)

Above and overleaf: Victories and Awards achieved by pilots and aircrew of the RAF Squadrons based at RAF Little Snoring. Bertie is mentioned numerous times on these score boards, which were painted by Corporal Douglas Higgins, an airman who was stationed at the airfield. (Author's Collection)

Victories

Date	Squadron	Name	Place	Claim
20.8.44	515	F/Lt Callard F/S Townsley	Prion	2 Do 24 Destroyed
20.8.44	515	F/Lt Callard F/S Townsley	Friedburg	Me 109 Destroyed
20.8.44	515	S/L Morley F/S Fidler	Holzkirchen	2 SI 204, Damaged
20.9.44	515	S/L Morley F/S Fidler	Munich Neubiberg A/F	Ju 88 Damaged
22.10.44	515	F/Lt L'Amie F/O Smith J.	Strasburg Area	Ju 34 Destroyed
22.10.44	515	F/Lt L'Amie F/O Smith J.	Prague Area	3 Me 109, Destroyed
22.10.44	515	F/Lt L'Amie F/O Smith J.	Prague Area	2 Me 109, Damaged
22.10.44	515	P/O Groves F/S Dockeray	Ingolstadt	Me 110 Destroyed
22.10.44	515	P/O Groves F/S Dockeray	Prague Area	3 Me 109, Destroyed
22.10.44	515	P/O Groves F/S Dockeray	Prague Area	3 Me 109, Damaged
22.10.44	515	W/C Lambert F/O Lake	Grossenbrode A/F	Unidentified Destroyed
4.11.44	23	F/O Stewart F/O Beaudet	Ardorf A/F	Ju 88 Damaged
4.11.44	23	F/O Stewart F/O Beaudet	Ardorf A/F	He 111 Damaged
18.11.44	23	F/Lt Badley F/S Wilson	Veerlosse A/F	3 Ju 88 Damaged
28.11.44	23	F/Lt Smith F/O Cockayne	Echterdingen A/F	2 Unidentified Damaged
28.11.44	23	F/Lt Smith F/O Cockayne	Eutingen A/F	Ju 88 Damaged
2.12.44	515	F/O Huls F/O Kinet	Fassberg A/F	He 177 Destroyed
2.12.44	515	F/O Huls F/O Kinet	Fassberg A/F	He 177 Damaged
22.12.44	515	W/C Kelsey F/O Smith E.M.	Rosenborn A/F	He 111 Damaged
24.12.44	515	W/C Kelsey F/O Smith E.M.	Rosenborn A/F	Ju 52 Damaged
22.12.44	515	W/C Kelsey F/O Smith E.M.	Rosenborn A/F	Ju 88 Damaged
22.12.44	515	S/L Bennett F/Lt Smith	Lin Fiord	Ju 88 Destroyed
1.1.45	23	S/L Tweedale F/Lt Cunningham	Alhorn Area	Ju 88 Destroyed
5.1.45	515	F/Lt Briggs F/O Rodwell	Jagel A/F	Ju 88 Destroyed
14.1.45	23	F/Lt Smith F/O Cockayne	Gutersloh A/F	Unidentified Destroyed
3.2.45	515	W/C Kelsey F/O Smith E.M.	Veckfa Area	Ju 88 Destroyed
22.2.45	515	W/O Adams F/S Widdicombe	Bonn A/F	Ju 88 Damaged
6.3.45	515	F/O Bartlam F/O Harvey	Griefswald A/F	Ju 52 Damaged
8.3.45	515	F/O Bartlam F/O Harvey	Griefswald A/F	Unidentified Damaged
8.3.45	515	F/O Bartlam F/O Harvey	Barth A/F	Unidentified Damaged
10.3.45	23	F/Lt Smith F/O Cockayne	Fassberg A/F	Me 109 Destroyed
10.3.45	23	F/Lt Smith F/O Cockayne	Fassberg A/F	Me 109 Damaged
7.3.45	23	F/O Heath F/S Thompson	Stendal	Fw 190 Destroyed
10.3.45	23	S/L O'Brien F/L Dinny	N.E. Fassberg	Ju 88 Damaged
12.3.45	3110	Station Browning Battery	Little Snoring A/F	Ju 88 Damaged
21.3.45	515	F/O Huls F/O Kinet	Buch A/F	FW 190 Destroyed
24.3.45	515	P/O Adams F/S Widdicombe	Erding A/F	Unidentified Destroyed
24.3.45	515	P/O Adams F/S Widdicombe	Erding A/F	4 Unidentified Damaged
22.3.45	23	F/O Field F/S Gilbertson	Crailsheim A/F	Me 109 probably Destroyed
30.3.45	515	P/O Holland F/S Young	Nordholz A/F	Me 210 Destroyed
30.3.45	515	P/O Holland F/S Young	Nordholz A/F	2 Me 210, Damaged
1.4.45	515	P/O Adams F/S Widdicombe	Erding A/F	Me 110 Damaged
4.4.45	23	F/S Goody F/S Jacobs	Rechlin A/F	Unidentified Damaged
4.4.45	515	P/O Holland F/S Young	Schleissheim Area	Ju 52 Destroyed
24.4.45	515	W/O Mallows W/O Gostelow	Lista A/F	Unidentified Damaged
24.4.45	23	W/O East F/S Eames	Lista A/F	Ju 188 Destroyed
24.4.45	515	W/C Kelsey F/Lt Smith	Prague	Do 217 Destroyed
24.4.45	515	F/Lt Davis F/O Cronin	Kaufbeurn A/F	8 Unidentified Damaged

xvi

Honours & Awards

Date	Squadron	Name	Awards
Aug. 1943	115	Sergeant Rosenbloom	D.F.M.
Sep. 1943	115	Squadron Leader Starkey	D.S.O.
Sep. 1943	115	Flying Officer Beer	D.F.C.
Sep. 1943	115	Flight Sergeant Anderson	D.F.M.
Sep. 1943	115	Sergeant Willis	D.F.M.
Sep. 1943	115	Sergeant Tugwell	D.F.M.
Nov. 1943	115	Flight Sergeant Rogers	D.F.M.
Nov. 1943	115	Warrant Officer Darby	D.F.C.
Nov. 1943	115	Warrant Officer Boullier	D.F.C.
Jan. 1944	115	Pilot Officer Newton	D.F.C.
Jan. 1944	115	Pilot Officer Webb	D.F.C.
Jan. 1944	115	Pilot Officer Pipe	D.F.C.
Jan. 1944	115	Squadron Leader Annan	D.S.O.
Jan. 1944	S.H.Q.	L.a.c. Rout	Mention in Despatches
Jan. 1944	S.H.Q.	Warrant Officer Rollitt	Mention in Despatches
May 1944	160	Pilot Officer Miller	D.F.C.
May 1944	160	Pilot Officer Bone	D.F.C.
May 1944	160	Flight Lieutenant Woodman	D.F.C.
May 1944	160	Flight Lieutenant Kenmuis	D.F.C.
June 1944	515	Flying Officer Lake	A.F.C.
June 1944	S.H.Q.	Corporal Bate	Mention in Despatches
June 1944	S.H.Q.	L.a.c. Webster	Mention in Despatches
June 1944	S.H.Q.	Squadron Leader Price	Mention in Despatches
July 1944	515	Wing Commander Lambert	D.F.C.
July 1944	515	Flight Lieutenant Morgan D.F.C.	First Bar to D.F.C.
Sep. 1944	515	Flying Officer Newberry	D.F.C.
Oct. 1944	515	Flying Officer Chown	D.F.C.
Oct. 1944	515	Flight Lieutenant Adams	D.F.C.
Oct. 1944	515	Pilot Officer Ruffle	D.F.C.
Oct. 1944	515	Pilot Officer Groves	D.F.C.
Oct. 1944	515	Flying Officer Lake	D.F.C.
Oct. 1944	515	Pilot Officer Prested	D.F.C.
Oct. 1944	515	Flight Sergeant Verity	D.F.M.
Oct. 1944	515	Flight Sergeant Dockeray	D.F.M.
Nov. 1944	515	Squadron Leader Martin D.S.O. D.F.C.	Second Bar to D.F.C.
Nov. 1944	S.H.Q.	Flying Officer Vanderplassche	Mention in Despatches
Nov. 1944	23	Flight Lieutenant Badley	D.F.C.
Dec. 1944	515	Wing Commander Lambert D.F.C.	D.S.O.
Nov. 1944	515	Flight Lieutenant Callard	D.F.C.
Dec. 1944	23	Wing Commander Murphy D.S.O. D.F.C. c&a	First Bar to D.S.O.
Dec. 1944	515	Flight Lieutenant L'Amie	D.F.C.
Dec. 1944	515	Flying Officer Smith J. W.	D.F.C.
Dec. 1944	23	Warrant Officer Griffiths	D.F.C.
Dec. 1944	23	Warrant Officer Maude	D.F.C.
Jan. 1945	S.H.Q.	Group Captain Hoare D.S.O. D.F.C.	Mention in Despatches
Jan. 1945	S.H.Q.	Flight Lieutenant Forth	Mention in Despatches
Jan. 1945	515	Warrant Officer Ecclestone	Mention in Despatches
Jan. 1945	S.H.Q.	Squadron Leader Price	O.B.E.
Jan. 1945	23	Warrant Officer Collinson	M.B.E.
Jan. 1945	23	Flight Sergeant Parker	Mention in Despatches
Jan. 1945	23	Flight Sergeant Stephens	Mention in Despatches
Jan. 1945	515	Flight Sergeant Slade	Mention in Despatches
Jan. 1945	515	Sergeant Paling Slater	Mention in Despatches
Jan. 1945	9903 S.E.	Corporal Chapman	Mention in Despatches
Jan. 1945	S.H.Q.	Corporal Mc K. Craig	Mention in Despatches
Jan. 1945	515	Corporal Kirkpatrick	Mention in Despatches
Jan. 1945	515	L.a.c. Collins	Mention in Despatches
Jan. 1945	515	L.a.c. Hole	Mention in Despatches

EARLY LIFE

Bertie Rex O'Bryen Hoare was born on 6 June 1912, Hove, East Sussex. He was the only son of Cyril Bertie Edward O'Bryen Hoare and Isabel Mary Fielder. His older sister, Hermione Sophia O'Bryen Hoare was two years his senior, born on 27 February 1910.

Bleak House. (Courtesy of Booth Museum and David Fisher)

His father, a man of local stature by profession, was recorded in the 1911, *The Plantagenet Roll of the Royal Blood, Volume 1*, through the Mortimer-Percy ancestry blood line, as being a close descendant of King Edward III. The family home was 195 Dyke Road, Hove, known as Bleak House; it was a large suburban house built in the mid-nineteenth century by Edward Thomas Booth, who was known as the founder of the museum of 'British Birds', which was erected on the grounds of the estate, and still is in existence today. The family house was demolished in the mid-twentieth century and later replaced by a block of flats named Fairlawn. The family moved from Bleak House in 1918 to D'Avigdor House, a substantive sized suburban house originally built in 1903 for the Parsons family.

Bertie had a comfortable childhood growing up on the south coast of England, enjoying country pastimes including fishing, tennis, and shooting. Another hobby of his was magic, which he enjoyed throughout his life; as a young boy he often entertained family and friends with tricks and illusions.

From 1926 to 1930 Bertie attended Harrow Boys' School, Middlesex. Here, he was noted as a strong sportsman, representing his schoolhouse, Rendell's, in Boxing, after his mother told him 'he must learn

A view looking south, just outside Booth's Bird Museum. The high wall beyond enclosed Bleak House. (Courtesy of regencysociety.org)

to defend himself'. He also played Rugby, in the full-back position. His schoolmaster commented, 'Hoare's greatness is his love of fair play, his enthusiasm, and his team spirit.' In his later teenage years he attended South-Eastern Agricultural College, at Wye in Kent, between October 1930 – July 1932, where he gained a certificate in agriculture.

The front cover of a box which contained one of Bertie's many magic tricks. (Courtesy of R. Russell and E. Eyre)

South-Eastern Agricultural College, Wye, Kent, which Bertie attended and obtained a college certificate in Agricultural. (Courtesy of Wye Agricola Club)

DRURIES v. THE GROVE.

This match was played on A.Wy.'s second ground under conditions which favoured the heavy Druries side, who won 11—1. Druries played up hill and against the wind. The Grove backs kicked well and Druries could only score twice before half-time. Willis scored for The Grove with a good ground shot, bringing the score to 2—1 at half-time. In the second half the Druries forwards were too strong for the Grove defence and scored several times, the score at the end of the match being 11—1.

For the winners Couper and Phipps played well, and for the losers Willis and Sharpe were the best.

Druries: D. O. Couper, M. C. S. Phipps, N. R. Grimston, F. B. Peel, G. Brown, A. S. R. Gascoyne, H. L. Hole, G. W. G. Threlfall, R. C. Cox, A. Shorland-Hall, J. G. Bedford.

The Grove: J. G. S. Hobson, H. G. Willis, E. C. Sharpe, W. Wormald, C. P. Green, H. Coke, N. A. Mardon, W. H. Openshaw, J. S. M. Booth, C. H. F. Walker, T. T. Casdagli.

BRADBYS v. SMALL HOUSES AND HOME BOARDERS.

This match, played on A.W.S.'s ground, was won by Bradbys by 2 bases to 1 after a good hard game on a sticky and tiring ground. Bradbys won the toss and played down, soon being rewarded by a base by Seligman. de Clermont later scored a second. Bradbys lost a good centre in de Rougemont at this point, but just managed to prevent their opponents scoring more than once, by Collins.

Bradbys: P. H. V. de Clermont, (R. G. Pegler), J. W. A. Duckworth, R. A. D. de Rougemont, P. W. Seligman, G. B. Hunter, N. W. Vickers, R. H. Wright, A. C. Sturge, M. B. Evans, A. S. Harman, R. B. Collie and H. K. Wright.

Small Houses and Home Boarders: C. D. Van Namen, J. B. T. Collins, J. A. F. McKay, A. Shahinian, B. C. Berger, D. W. Poppel, J. D. Spinney, The Maharajah of Bhavnagar, S. R. Das, G. Booth, G. Gonwy.

THE PARK v. RENDALLS.

The Park, who won 1—0, played uphill first half. Play was very even in this half, neither side being able to score. In the second half The Park soon pressed and Nichols scored with a shot off the ground. Despite dangerous rushes by the Rendalls forwards The Park contrived to hold the advantage and should have scored two or three times more.

Benn for the winners, and Poke, who was very outstanding, and Blackmore, for the losers, were the best.

The Park: D. A. T. Tangye (capt.), A. Benn, P. K. Crowther, C. D. Laborde, W. R. Nichols, I. A. Macmillan, K. D. Laborde, H. E. Chubb, T. J. Taylor, G. F. D. Haslewood, R. H. Russell.

Rendalls: H. Blackmore (capt.), A. Chamberlain, J. M. F. Lightly, C. D. Norman-Barnett, J. C. Wade, B. R. O. Hoare, G. J. Poke, J. D. Harrison, R. Fox, T. F. Hartley, V. E. Laroque.

SECOND ROUND.

BRADBYS v. HEADMASTER'S (B).

Bradbys won the toss and played down hill and won the match 8—0. The ground (A.Wy.'s) was sticky and tiring. Sturge opened their score with a good shot off yards. de Clermont then added three more. After half-time Bradbys again had most of the game, and further bases came from Hunter, Collie, Duckworth and Seligman. The centres were well together and showed plenty of dash and spirit, though much smaller than their opponents. Seligman and de Clermont played very well. The H.M.(b) went hard, but were not so well together and lacked a strong back.

Bradbys: P. H. V. de Clermont, (R. G. Pegler), J. W. A. Duckworth, R. A. D. de Rougemont, P. W. Seligman, N. W. Vickers, G. B. Hunter, R. H. Wright, A. C. Sturge, M. B. Evans, R. B. Collie, H. K. Wright.

Headmaster's (B): P. L. Lewis, H. B. Relton, H. W. Churchill, J. M. Jennings, A. V. D. Gordon, M. G. Burrows, Prince Bhanu, R. B. Verney, M. J. Armstrong, F. P. Trehearne, A. E. Hill.

Extract taken from the Harrovian, 31 March 1928, showing a result of a Rugby match which Bertie played in. (Courtesy of Harrow School)

Enjoying the countryside. (Courtesy of R. Russell)

Above: Hermione enjoying a walk with her brother. (Courtesy of R. Russell)

Opposite above: Aviation ran in the family, here Hermione takes flight in a Slingsby Falcon III, which was produced from 1935 to 1938, with nine being built. The glider with Hermione in the photo probably belonged to the London Gliding Club, Dunstable (the little round patch on the nose cross-references with other photos). A Falcon III (possibly this one) was used at Dunstable to set up a world soaring-duration record of twenty-two hours in 1938, the Germans unfortunately raised it to over fifty hours later that year. (Courtesy of D. Fisher)

Opposite below: A newspaper cutting showing Hermione preparing to take off in a glider. Hermione was nicknamed Bones, due to her weight gain when attempting to swim the English channel. Later, with Bertie's tragic death, she became skinny with grief. (Courtesy of D. Fisher)

MISS HERMIONE HOARE IN HER GLIDING GARMENT

cool fashion exhibited when the Oxford University Gliding Club
ere under canvas on a recent occasion. Miss Hoare is one of
s most enthusiastic members; is also captain of the Oxford
niversity women's swimming team and an English International
-hockey player. Gliding, to the uninitiated, seems as if it might
spice more danger than either lion-taming or steeple-chasing

COMMISSIONED INTO THE
ROYAL AIR FORCE

1936

Bertie received a short service commission, attaining the rank of acting Pilot Officer on probation with seniority date of 18 May 1936, gazetted in the *London Gazette* on 2 June 1936. His mother recalls, 'he saw trouble ahead, and determined that when war came it would find him ready and that's why he joined the RAF.'

Bertie completed his initial flying training at No.3 Elementary and Reserve Flying Training School Hamble, Hampshire, between 23 March to 18 May 1936, receiving a flying aptitude grading of 81 per cent. He progressed to No.11 Flying Training School at RAF Wittering, Cambridgeshire, commencing his course on 2 June. 11 FTS was formed on 1 October 1935, with its first flying course commencing on 4 November the same year. Some senior RAF officers reported the standard of flying at the school was the best in the world. Consisting of two squadrons, the first was for flying training, and trained pilots such as Bertie to become satisfactory pilots in the best practice of airmanship. The second was an advanced training squadron which trained pilots to meet a rudimentary RAF level before being posted to an operational squadron. Training aircraft included Avro Tutors, Hawker Audaxes, and Harts. September 1936 saw the introduction of Gloster Gauntlets and Hawker Furies.

RAF Wittering hosted many VIPs, and one such occasion was on 8 July 1936, when HM King Edward VIII, and his brother, the Duke of York, and the Chief of the Air Staff, Air Chief Marshal Sir Edward Ellington visited. The visit was also historic for the King, flying his scarlet and blue Rapide aircraft from his private airfield at Windsor Great Park, Berkshire, to RAF Northolt, Hillingdon. Finally, flying on to RAF Wittering to become Britain's first 'flying' King.

On 29 October 1937 a Luftwaffe mission paid a visit to RAF Wittering to inspect the training system. The party consisted of seven German senior

HM King Edward VIII, conducting an inspection of RAF Wittering with his Royal party on 8 July 1936. (Courtesy of RAF Archives)

Generalleutnant Hans Jurgen Stumf (Chief of the General Staff – Luftwaffe) 15 June 1889 – 9 March 1968. A First World War soldier, becoming head of personnel in the Luftwaffe on 1 September 1933. During the Second World War he commanded various Luftlotten. Taking part in the Battle of Britain in 1940, he commanded Luftlotte 5, operating from Norway. Stumf served as a Luftwaffe representative at the signing of the unconditional surrender of Germany in Berlin on 8 May 1945. (Courtesy of WW2 Talk forum)

officers and three British officers. The German party included General des Fliegers, Erhard Milch (Secretary of State of Aviation), Generalleutnant Hans Jurgen Stumf (Chief of the General Staff), and Generalmajor Ernst Udet (Director of the Technical Department), all playing future important roles in the Third Reich.

To train a raw pilot was not without risks, remembered by Flight Lieutenant Edwin Shipley in 1937, a flying instructor with 11 FTS.

> On November 4th we had a programme arranged of that dangerous practice of night flying. The night flying practice was quite well for a while. We had no radios on the Harts and all the instructions from the ground were given by coloured Aldis lamps. Then quite suddenly a November fog started to blow up and we hastily recalled all aircraft that were airborne. They all got back but one, and this we could hear droning around above the fog as the instructor had decided that it was, by then, unsafe to attempt a landing. By this time the fog had got quite thick but was obviously only a hundred feet or less in height and we assumed that they would fly around to burn off fuel and then abandon the aircraft. So, we settled for a long wait. To enable them to keep their bearing on Wittering, we touched off a rocket or a maroon every two or three minutes and this was successful as they kept circuiting the aerodrome.
>
> It was realised that the demand on pyrotechnics was going to be considerable and the duty armourer was dispatched to get more from the long-term storage. Well, more than an hour later we heard the engine cut out and metaphorically put our umbrellas up! The next thing we knew was that all the lights went out. Now I do not mean some, but all the lights in the Soke of Peterborough, and this created a minor panic to switch on car headlights and the like. The pupil had landed on high-tension cables and said later that he was there for what seemed a lifetime while a sort of Brock's Benefit went on above him. He said that he had difficulty in making the decision on whether to stay there and be electrocuted, or to bang his quick release and fall, risking breaking a leg, or more. He did the latter but only fell about two feet – and ran like hell. The instructor came

down in the garden of a public house in Collyweston as the door opened to release a crowd of lads out into the fog. He had great difficulty convincing them that he had just landed by parachute when he asked where he was, until he showed them the parachute.

The aircraft had come down quite quietly in a field and they had some difficulty in locating it the following day. You can understand that the bonfire night on the following day fell a little flat particularly as the major contribution planned, that of outdated service pyrotechnics, just was not there.

Bertie successfully completed his basic flying training 22 August, and was presented with the coveted RAF wings. His final report concluded: 'An average pilot, steady and reliable officer.'

Wing Commander Roderick Alastair Brook Learoyd, recipient of the Victoria Cross, was a fellow pilot 'under training' with Bertie at 11 FTS, RAF Wittering in 1936. (IWM Collections)

Above left: A young Pilot Officer Bertie Hoare wearing his RAF No.1 dress uniform, photographed in late 1936 on completion of his initial training and passing out as a RAF officer. (Courtesy of R. Russell)

Above right: Bertie's nickname originated from his uncle, Sir Samuel Hoare, 2nd Baronet, also called (from 1944) Viscount Templewood of Chelsea. Coming back into the government after retirement in June 1936 as first lord of the admiralty and then, in May 1937, under Neville Chamberlain, as home secretary. As one of the inner councils that developed the Munich Pact, he became one of its staunchest defenders, further marking him as an appeaser, to the ultimate damage of his reputation. After war broke out and Churchill became prime minister in 1940, Hoare's parliamentary service was at an end. During the war (1940–44) he served as ambassador to Spain. In 1944 he was created Viscount Templewood and shortly thereafter retired from public life. (Courtesy of Britannica)

A PROFESSIONAL FLYING CLUB

1937–40

Between the world wars the Royal Air Force was fighting for its survival, with some military commanders asking whether there was a need for a separate Air Force to exist in peacetime. If these senior officers could only foresee what a great contribution and human sacrifice this service made throughout the forthcoming events of the Second World War.

Bomber Command was formed on 14 July 1936 with its Headquarters at RAF Uxbridge, Hillingdon. At the time it was believed that a strong bomber force would be a deterrent to any enemy aggression as this force could deliver complete inescapable destruction against any adversaries. Air Marshal John Steel, originally a Royal Navy pilot who had learnt to fly at the age of 40, having transferred to the Royal Air Force on its birth on 1 April 1918, worked his way through senior command and staff positions, taking command of Air Defence Great Britain (ADGB), the primary purpose of which was the defence of the British Isles. The ADGB was made up of three defensive zones across the British Isles, each operating in areas strategically positioned around London and the Sussex coastline; it consisted of a layered Anti-Aircraft screen and fighter aircraft coverage which could be deployed at short notice to act against any unfriendly intervention. This ADGB was disbanded on 13 July 1936 with Air Marshal Steel taking over Bomber Command the next day.

One squadron that was incorporated into Bomber Command was 207 Squadron, re-forming at RAF Bircham Newton, Norfolk, on 1 February 1920. Initially flying Airco DH.9As, its official motto in Latin reads, *Semper paratus*, translating to 'Always prepared'. Its unofficial nickname was the 'Black Cats', due to the design on the squadron's crest (see overleaf).

207 squadron arrived at RAF Cottesmore, Rutland, on 20 April 1938 from RAF Worthy Down, Hampshire, where they retired their ageing Vickers Wellesley aircraft and were refitted with Fairey Battles and a small number of Avro Anson Mark 1 aircraft.

On 9 January 1937 a new pilot, No 37853 Acting Pilot Officer Bertie Hoare, arrived at 207 Squadron, then based at RAF Worthy Down, and immediately joined A Flight. It was not long until he was flying routine training sorties, as recorded in the squadron log: 'attending numerous armament practice camps and aerial bombing across the United Kingdom'. On 11 October he flew a Vickers Wellesley aircraft to RAF Scampton, Lincolnshire, where he was joined by two other aircraft, flown by Flying Officers Peter Fleming and Phillip Harrington. The formation completed a flypast for visiting German army staff officers, and returned to their home airfield on the same day. Bertie attained the substantive rank of Pilot Officer on 23 March, gazetted in the *London Gazette* on 4 May 1937.

Bertie made squadron history on 17 December, recorded in the squadron log: 'One of the longest training sorties to RAF Aldergrove, long distance bombing exercise 5 hours 45 mins, first ever for this type of aircraft, pilot and observer appeared unduly fatigued on landing.' He took part in the squadron move to RAF Cottesmore in April 1938 and transitioned to a new aircraft, with pilots soon getting used to the modern Fairey Battle aircraft.

207 Squadron, RAF crest, its motto was *Semper Paratus*, 'Always Prepared'. (Courtesy of RAF Copyright)

RAF Worthy Down outside A Flight Office: L–R: Pilot Officers David 'Tosis' Halliday, Bertie, Henry 'Pluto' Angell, Anthony 'Popeye' Hudson, Neil 'Nebby' Wheeler, and Flying Officer Peter Fleming. (Courtesy of 207 Squadron Association)

L–R Pilot Officer Anthony 'Popeye Hudson', Flying Officer Peter Fleming, and Bertie Relaxing outside A Flight offices at 207 Squadron, RAF Worthy Down. (Courtesy of 207 Squadron Association)

Bertie completed a series of instructional courses, including a course at the School of Navigation, Shoreham, West Sussex, between 21 August and 11 November.

One of his closest friends at the squadron was Pilot Officer Henry Angell, nicknamed 'Pluto', he recalls RAF Cottesmore when 207 Squadron were based there.

> Cottesmore was not a particularly comfortable station at the time. The Ram Jam Inn at Stretton on the Great North Road was the focal point of a great deal of our social life. The Great North Road was also part of our flying, with its double line of telegraph poles, unique at the time I believe. For us this was a Navigational Landmark, especially when returning from the firing area in the Wash in poor visibility. We knew that at least we had not overshot Cottesmore and with a bit of 'Bradshawing', we could map read our way back to base.

Bertie also became close friends with the squadron Adjutant, Flying Officer Neil 'Nebby' Wheeler, and would have the honour to be the godfather to Neil's daughter. Wheeler would survive the Second World War, reaching the senior rank of Air Chief Marshal as Sir Neil Wheeler, retiring from the RAF in January 1976.

Bertie was promoted to the substantive rank of Flying Officer, with the seniority date of 23 September, gazetted in the *London Gazette* on 11 October 1938. Less than a year later, on 1 May 1939, he gained the rank of Acting Flight Lieutenant, gazetted in the *London Gazette* on 3 October 1939 and recorded in the squadron log on 24 August. 'A third flight will be formed shortly with Flying Officer B.R.O'B Hoare, as its commander.'

On 24 August, 207 Squadron moved from RAF Cottesmore to their new home at RAF Cranfield, Bedfordshire, with 35 Squadron following closely behind them, arriving on 25 August. 35 Squadron amalgamated with 207 Squadron to form No.1 Group Pool for training of personnel for Advanced Air Striking Force on 1 October 1940. The first training course commencing with a total of nine pilots, sixteen air observers and nine air gunners in attendance. Bertie was one of these pilots that attended the initial course and this was the start of Bertie's career to becoming a RAF Intruder ace.

Drawn by an unknown artist in 1939, Bertie is depicted driving a sports cars, bottom right. Pilot Officer Neil 'Nebby' Wheeler is standing top right wearing a prestige flying suit. (Courtesy of 207 Squadron Association)

RAF Cottesmore, Rutland, taken pre-war when 207 and 35 squadron were based here. (Courtesy of 207 Squadron Association)

L–R Pilot Officers, Unknown, Lewis Johnston, Henry 'Pluto' Angell, Bertie seated relaxing holding his dog, Tadzee (Courtesy of 207 Squadron Association)

Standing with his ground crew, Bertie is fifth from the left in front of a Fairey Battle aircraft. (Courtesy of 207 Squadron Association)

Photographed in July 1938, 207 Squadron pilots posing in front of Fairey Battle aircraft, Bertie is standing front row, sixth from left. (Courtesy of 207 Squadron Association)

Above left and above right: Tadzee, Bertie's faithful companion. This unusual name came from the Native American-Athabaskan language, which translates to 'the loon'. (Courtesy of R. Russell)

NELSON OF THE RAF

On the afternoon of 6 October 1939, Bertie was piloting a Mark 1 Fairey Battle. Serial No L4966, his passenger was Acting Sergeant Gerald Emery, from C Flight. Taking off from their home airfield at 14:45, both airmen were carrying out observer training. Leading Aircraftsman Nicholas Temperley, an aircraft mechanic, had prepared the aircraft for flying that day. The flight path was to take the aircraft around the local area and conduct a map exercise between 7,000ft and 9,000ft, four miles from RAF Cranfield. Bertie came up on his Receive and Transmit intercom, telling his Observer that he was going to decrease altitude at a speed of 200–270mph. Gently pushing the control stick forward, the aircraft's nose went into a shallow dive. Emery recalls:

> All of a sudden a crash, and the Perspex of a rear cockpit hood was smashed by some part of the aircraft becoming detached. I reported to the pilot, but there was no reply. I then asked the pilot if he was alright, he replied, 'I hope so'. And I noticed that his face was bleeding.

An engine cowling panel had detached itself from the aircraft and Bertie later reported that it 'smashed through left side of the windscreen and struck me in the face and I pulled the aircraft out of the dive at 3,500ft'. Miraculously, Bertie landed the damaged aircraft at 16:50 with his face full of blood, but still managed to taxi back towards the squadron hangar at Cranfield where LAC Temperley was waiting to receive them. Temperley could see something was not right however: 'It taxied on to the tarmac outside No.2 hangar, I saw that the port centre engine cowling was missing. After assisting the pilot from the cockpit, I immediately reported the matter to Flight Sergeant Browton, i/c Flight.'

Flight Sergeant Browton briefed the ground crew to immediately to shut down the aircraft's engine and aided the injured pilot out of the cockpit. He then transported him to the station sick quarters for treatment.

On 12 October the RAF carried out an internal investigation of the incident, led by Flight Lieutenant Richard Wardell and overseen by Group Captain Wilfred Dunn, the Station commander at Cranfield. The summary findings were released on 23 October, concluding:

> It is conclusive that F/O Hoare was on duty on the flight in question and the accident occurred through a part of the cowling becoming detached. The security of the cowling appears to have been checked and as the front sockets were undamaged, one can only presume the buttons must have fractured. The third witness states this is not the first time this has happened. I do not consider anyone to blame. The aircraft dived, causing an increase in pressure on the open end of the cowling and forcing it to be blown off. The speed attained by the aircraft in the dive was within the limitations of the Battle aircraft and if the cowling had been secure, the accident would never have happened.

It was reported from the initial medical treatment that Bertie was 'slightly' injured, sustaining only a broken nose. However, the blow he sustained to his head from the engine cowling hitting him impaired his vision and he was completely blinded in one eye for life. Later in his service career he received the nickname in the national newspapers and media as 'The RAF's Nelson'!

A more implausible account from an unknown squadron source says that Bertie was injured in flight when 'a duck flew through his windscreen and afterwards he had a glass eye, he had one brown eye, one blue eye, no-one seemed to know which was the glass one.'

A further squadron colleague commented on the accident and the damage and an assumption regarding the loss of Bertie's eye.

> Bertie took a hit in the face from a loose engine cowling. The resultant blow popped an eye out of its socket, and he landed due to his great skill and a bit of luck. Bertie was hospitalised for a six-month period. A very strange thing happened as a result of the accident. The injured eye now had amazing night vision capabilities.

DR   5528

Received S.1.(Tele) 1105 hours 12/10/39.

Telegram en clair to Air Ministry rptd. 6 Group,
from 207 Squadron Cranfield.

IMMEDIATE.

A.846 12/10.   F.A. (A) Battle L.4966. (B)
207. (C) 4 miles S.W. Cranfield 6/10/39 1500 hours. (D) 37853
A/P/Lt. B.R. O'B Hoare slightly injured broken nose. (E) N/A.

S.7.(Cas) informed by 'phone 1130 hours.

Time of Origin: 1005.

Copies to:-

S.of S.	D.H.O.
Parly.U.S. of S.	D.P.S.
C.A.S.	Permt. U.S. of S.
O.7.	2nd S.U.S.
D.O.R.	P.A.S.(P)
D.of Ops.(C.S.)	
D.C.A.S.	F.3.(2)
A.C.A.S.	E.1.
S.7.b.	A.2.(2)
S.7.(Cas)(2)(Action)	E.3.(2)
A.M.P.	S.4. Stats.
P.P.B.	I.of A.(Action)
D.of T.	Inspector General.
D.D.R.M.	Records Office Ruislip.

RECEIVED

12 OCT 1939

CASUALTY

An official RAF casualty document showing the extent of Bertie's injuries as only slight. (Courtesy of National Archives Kew)

207 Squadron Mark 1 Fairey Battles (B) K9185 and (C) K9186 similar to the model of aircraft that Bertie was flying when his flying accident occurred on 6 October 1939. (Courtesy of 207 Squadron Association)

With his sight lost in one eye he was sent to the RAF Hospital at RAF Henlow, Bedfordshire, to recover and wrote many letters home to his mother describing his emotions about not being able to fly.

> RAF Hospital
> Henlow
> Beds
> 11 November
>
> Dear Ma,
> First there isn't any news in brief worth speaking of. The hospital is as monotonously Noisy as ever; I am much better.
> Nurse Leper is much better.
> The weather is much better.
> Hitler is much better after his narrow escape.
> How is your bandstand now-a-days? Mine is much better, thank you.
> Yesterday I went for a short walk, and caught a rather long cold, I'm afraid, which is rather a nuisance as I am not allowed to go out now and have to wear my parachute outfit all the time now, which is a bit of a bore. Otherwise, life is much the same usual.
> Oh dear! Oh dear! Oh dear! My typing isn't all it might be, but people keep talking to me.

I am being moved to Halton next week and back again in the same day to see a man about an eye. I am trying to go to Huntercombe (Lord Nuffield's Golf Club or home, I hope the latter), but it is highly unlikely that I won't be allowed to.

I asked Peggy to write a letter for me and of course it is a lot of nonsense. Hermione and Peggy have been up here this week and cheered me up no end. I did get a bit of a cold the other day but it's better now thank goodness, on Sat I thought I was going to die, it was awful, and I hope neither the child of Peggy caught it, or Tadzee. Felix and his girlfriend also came over she has the longest nails I have ever seen.

About this business of coming home as Peggy has tried to say on Thursday I go to see the eye fellow and after that I should be able either to go home if that is allowed, or go to Huntercombe, and if I can get away on the Friday or the Sat Peggy will drive me down in the M.G., but if it's after the weekend I might want you to drive me if you could …. Then again of course I may have to stay here but I'll let you know anyway.

I hope this is lovely enough typing for you to read but I do it all in the dark with the use of even one eye, the eyes are getting along nicely now …..

Even if I go to Huntercombe now I expect that I shall get a few weeks sick leave afterwards and come home.

That's very good news about Jilly, it will save a lot of trouble and certainly shows that you can do it … I am very pleased to hear about the cabbage plants you will be very glad of them even if the water does end.

I've got a new wireless set with a short-wave band on it and I've just been listening to a broadcast from America of the whole XX records, very good only thing was a little bit of interference.

Sorry to hear the butter not good, ours is alright try getting it from your milk man or dairy who makes it. Bring a drum by all means, I'll be able to let you have some.

Bye bye all love
Rex

RAF Hospital
Henlow
Beds

Dear Ma,

It now seems rather likely that I shall be coming home over the weekend sometime. You wanted to know I advance so I am telling you but for goodness sake DO NOT go and make any special arrangements or I shall be very cross. I live like any ordinary person on ordinary food so don't bother about cooking difficulties any old food is ok for me ... If you don't treat me like an ordinary man I shall be most offended and shan't come home ....

I expect I shall get Peggy to drive me down in the M.G. as I shall want it at home anyway, but if that can't be managed I'll let you know.

I saw the eye Waller today and there seems to be little difference in it yet and rest is the only thing.

Bye bye all love
Rex

Lord and Lady Nuffield in the late 1930s. Viscount Nuffield, purchased Huntercombe Golf Club in 1926 and ran it as a sole proprietor until he sold it to the Members in 1963. (Courtesy of Huntercombe Golf Course)

Once fully recovered from his injuries, Bertie was grounded due to his poor eyesight, reluctantly accepting a staff appointment on 19 June as personal assistant to Air Marshal Sir Lawrence Arthur Pattinson, whose primary role was to oversee the RAF Training Command structure. This often required travelling together by aircraft to various RAF airfields, Bertie would be allowed to unofficially sit in the cockpit and fly.

Not content with staff duties and desperate to get back to operational flying, Bertie was reported as giving the medical authorities, 'no peace until they pronounced his sight with one eye, well above average.' Rumour has it

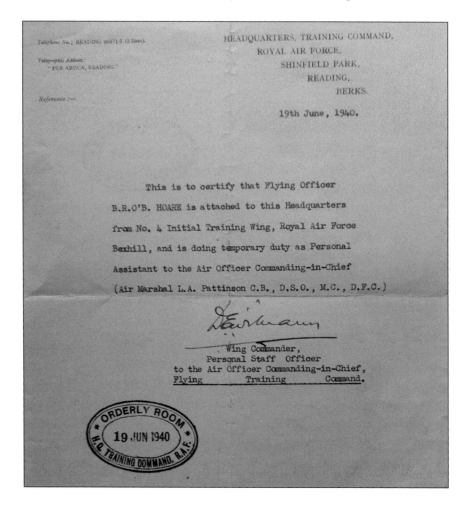

An official document confirming Bertie's short-term posting to No.4 Initial Training Wing. (Courtesy of RAF Historical Branch)

In 1940 Bertie was posted as ADC to Air Marshal Sir Lawrence Arthur Pattinson, KBE, CB, DSO, MC, DFC, who became Air Officer Commanding-in-Chief of Flying Training Command between 1940 to 1941. (Courtesy of RAF Museum Hendon)

that he got the Medical Officer drunk at an official function and got him to sign off his medical category there and then to allow him to fly once again.

A special report was written to the Air Ministry on 5 August.

Report A57664/40

Informed that in view of his recent examination at No.3 C.M.E where he was classified as fit for limited flying duties and ground duties only, he would normally be invalided from the service. The AASF decided however not to take that step at present, but to retain for employment within his present medical category, subject to review from time to time in the light of his medical reports, the requirement of the service, and any other relevant circumstances.

Recently found to be fit for full flying duties of his branch, when examined at the C.M.E (London) on 27-10-40, his name has been removed from the list of officers mentioned in the service is sufficient to periodic review.

Three medical forms confirming Bertie returning to flying training and posting to an operational squadron. (Courtesy of RAF Historical Branch)

FLIGHT COMMANDER
23 SQUADRON

1941

Promoted to a substantive rank of Flight Lieutenant on 3 September, gazetted in the *London Gazette* on 12 November 1940, Bertie was posted to 23 Squadron in January 1941 as a Flight Commander with B Flight. Since 12 September the previous year, 23 Squadron was based at RAF Ford, West Sussex, initially flying Bristol Blenheim aircraft. Due to the aircraft's slow speed and light armour it was ineffective as a night fighter. March and April saw the arrival of the American A-20 Douglas Havoc. Introduced into service with the squadron, the A-20 initially carried out endurance testing and operational performance before being brought into frontline operations. The Havoc was a medium range bomber and the night Intruder variant of the Boston aircraft, armed with a glazed nose, five 0.30-inch machine guns and a total payload of 2400lb bombs.

PLAYER'S CIGARETTES

No. 23 (FIGHTER) SQUADRON, R.A.F.

23 Squadron, RAF crest, its motto reads *Semper Aggressus*, Ever in the Attack. (Courtesy of RAF Copyright)

23 Squadron's primary role was to conduct night Intruder operations and to locate and destroy enemy bombers that were returning to their home bases. Intruder aircraft would lead their foe into a false sense of security by swooping out of the darkness and attack both aircraft and airfield.

Bertie did not have long to relax into squadron life; according to the 23 Squadron log, his first Intruder sortied was carried out on 20 February, in a Bristol Blenheim *B-Beer*. The target was German ground positions around Abbeville in Northern France. He conducted a similar type sortie on 3 March, flying Bristol Blenheim *T-Toc*; his Navigator was Pilot Officer Peter Morris and his Air Gunner Sergeant Walter Fletcher. They took off from RAF Manston, Kent, with four other Blenheim aircraft; their target was to attack Luftwaffe aircraft returning to their home airfields in the Northern French regions of Poix, Ameins, Beauvais, and Merville. The following is Bertie's personal account from this sortie:

> On ETA. I came down through 9/10 – 10/10 cloud, 8000ft, down to 2500ft. And saw an aerodrome with a double flare path, numerous red boundary lights. A searchlight shining down the flare path and numerous lights from a badly blacked out town to the South of the aerodrome which must have been Lille Nord. We orbited for about 15 minutes and saw a E/A with a large wingspan, burning navigation lights approaching to land. We dived to 2500ft astern of the E/A and fired a burst into the middle of the fuselage and his lights immediately went out. We passed over the E/A at about 50ft and dropped four bombs in front of him as he was finishing his landing run. All the aerodrome lights went out and intense light flak came up from all round the aerodrome, we used evasive action and got out of this, but on making a further circuit of the aerodrome we were caught in a searchlight and an even greater quantity of flak came up exceedingly close, but we were now at 2500ft. So, climbed steeply into the clouds and out of the searchlight.
>
> Rounds fired: 416
> Bombs: 4x 20lb bombs
> Length of burst: 275yds approx with a 3–4 second burst

This was Bertie's first claim and he was credited with a 'probable' for this engagement, the squadron log, however, stated 'damaged'. Official Luftwaffe reports record that a He 111 from Stab III./KG 53 carried out a force landing at Lille-Vendeville at the time receiving 35 per cent damage to its fuselage. However, it cannot be verified that it was connected to this engagement. Morris recalls this sortie in a letter he wrote to Bertie's mother after the war:

> I had the good fortune to be posted as a P/O Navigator to 23 Squadron at Ford in February 1941. I was crewed up, 'Sammy' as he was known to the squadron. I am proud to say that we both did our first operational flight together in Blenheim T. I was also with him when he bagged his first probable at 'Little Nord'. Afterwards, our path diverged I was posted from the squadron, but I always cherished this short but good association with him.

Sergeant Walter Thomas Fletcher, Bertie's Air Gunner on the Intruder sortie that was carried out on 3 March 1941 against Nord Lille airfield. (Courtesy of Battle of Britain London Monument)

On the night of 9 March Bertie took off from RAF Ford, again flying Bristol Blenheim, *T-Toc,* with his crew of skilled SNCOs, Sherrington and Fletcher. Flying low over the French countryside they observed a German vehicle convoy moving slow under the cover of darkness on the main road between the French cities of Goderville and Bolbec. Manoeuvring his aircraft as low as he could to 150ft, Bertie was well in the range of small arms fire. The vehicles, hearing the roar of the Blenheim's engine, immediately dispersed for cover. It was too late for some of these however; the Blenheim released 4 x 40lb bombs against its targets. Flying at such a low altitude on their return to their home airfield, the Blenheim received a flat tyre from fragments from the explosion of its own bombs, along with a hole in the wing and further damage to the aircraft's flying control column.

Good fortune continued on the night of 21 April. Flying Bristol Blenheim *T-Toc,* with the same crew as at the beginning of the month, Bertie took off with two other aircraft from RAF Manston, crossing the French coast over Gravelines, close to Dunkirk at an altitude of 10,000ft. Setting a navigational course for Lille airfield, they had no success in observing enemy aircraft so continued to fly to Achiet, another Luftwaffe airfield close

23 Squadron personnel, September 1941, Bertie standing in the centre, note the Bristol Blenheim parked inside the hangar behind the group. (Courtesy of R. Russell)

Sergeant Roy Claude
Sherrington flew on Bertie's
crew for a number of sorties.
He was awarded a DFM on
22 June 1942. He was lost in
action over Malta serving with
23 Squadron on 28 April 1943,
having flown fifty combat
operations. (Courtesy of
Chelmsford, WW2)

by attacking targets at Douai
and St Léger en route. Two
bomber-sized aircraft were
sighted at St Léger circling
the airfield. Bertie took his
aircraft to investigate whether
he could add to his tally.
Both enemy aircraft had their
landing lights on, the lead
aircraft was observed firing
four red star flares and then landed. The second aircraft had not noticed Bertie
manoeuvring his aircraft quietly behind on its tail at 1,000ft. The Blenheim
fired a total of 162 rounds from 50yds astern and below with a short burst
of cannon fire into the aircraft's belly. Bertie saw it was an exceptional size,
with a single rudder and slim appearance, noticing four exhaust stubs in a
straight line below the main plane. The remaining Blenheim crew reported
a slight difference and after the event one of the crew members said he saw
eight engine stubs on the target aircraft.

All of a sudden there was an almighty explosion as the parts of the stricken
aircraft disintegrated. Bertie's combat report records that 'fragments flew
past the Blenheim on all sides, burning pieces were strewn over a wide area
on the ground and flames were still seen from 25 to 30 miles away'.

The rear gunner's Perspex also received damage from the close proximity
of the explosion. Turning course for home, they left the French coast and
landed back at RAF Manston. The crew were tired but glad to be back at
their home airfield after their close encounter with the enemy aircraft. They
were also shocked to see that the tail and port wing of their aircraft had

received large fragmentation holes, including a 3ft piece of armoured plate embedded within it. Recalling this engagement in a letter home he writes:

> As at Ford … You say I never tell you what I am doing, so here is a real piece of news for you. It made me really quite excited! A wing and a trip I had last night. I heard of a new aerodrome the Hun was using, and got permission to go over there directly, it was dark. I bombed one aerodrome on the way, and when I found my target there was two Huns circling around, one very large, and one small. I picked the large, nipped in and fired a short burst, he exploded with a terrific flash and crashed in flames. The first four-engine job shot down at night, I believe. Maybe you heard it on the wireless this morning at 8? Bits of him hit me all over the place, or rather my aeroplane, and one bit stuck in the wing all the way home.
>
> I bought Tadzee home here, by air. His first trip, he looked a bit puzzled at first, oh boss, where are we now! But he slept on my coat all the way.

Bertie was credited with a 'destroyed' for this action, logging it as a Focke-Wulf 200 Condor transport plane. However, it was more likely to be Ju 88 A-5, Werk Nummer 5198. This aircraft was from unit IV./KG 1. Official Luftwaffe reports stated it crashed in the French region of Rosières. This aircraft was crewed by Feldwebel Erich Weber, Unteroffizier's Wilhelm Peters, Arno Otto, and Gefreiter Walemar Stallmacht, all were killed in this engagement.

Late over the night of 3–4 May Bertie had a lucky escape from a prowling Luftwaffe night fighter aircraft that carried out exactly the same manoeuvre against him that he had performed only two weeks earlier when he shot down the Ju 88. He was flying Havoc *D-Don* over occupied France, part of a four aircraft formation that had taken off from RAF Ford. Having evaded searchlights around various Luftwaffe airfields, they arrived at Le Bourget airfield close to Paris. Enemy aircraft were observed firing red flares into the sky and Bertie quickly saw one of the aircraft preparing to land, the Havoc turned towards its prey.

> We chased him and got within range as he was making his approach to land at 800 feet. I made a quarter attack from

BIG RAIDER SHOT DOWN IN FRANCE

It is learned in London that, during the night, a four-engined bomber was shot down by our night fighters over an aerodrome in Northern France.

The bomber, probably one of the Focke-Wulf Condor or Kurier types was not, it is believed, taking part in the night raids on this country. These machines, which have an exceptionally long range, are used for attacks on our merchant shipping far out in the Atlantic.

This is the first recorded "bag" by our night fighters of a machine of this type. Further details are expected later.

Above left: A newspaper article from *The Evening News*, dated 22 April 1941, documenting the engagement of a Fw 200. (Courtesy of RAF Historical Branch)

Above right: Gefreiter Walemar Stallmacht, KIA on 21 April 1941, he is buried at Bourdon War Cemetery, France. (Courtesy of Gunter Hartwich)

slightly above and opened fire at about 150 yds, closing to about 10 yds, and fired a 7 second burst which could be seen hitting the starboard engine and fuselage.

Proceeding to fly low over the stricken bomber at only 10ft, Bertie and his crew saw it was a Ju 88; Fletcher fired a further 3½ second burst of machine gun fire into the aircraft's port engine. It went into a vertical nosedive, but they did not see it crash. Bertie took his Havoc back up to the safety of 7,000ft and circled the now darkened airfield. Ffifteen minutes later the lights came back on and the Havoc went over the Luftwaffe airfield once again to cause more destruction; it dropped all its payload onto the runway, which was later reported as 'large fires were caused'. The lights immediately went back out, but the aircraft were still attempting to land; decreasing his aircraft's altitude to 1,000ft, Bertie saw a He 111 preparing to land, with its navigation lights on, firing red star flares in succession.

> I then closed into 150yds and opened fire from astern and a little to starboard and fired a 6 second burst which could be seen hitting the starboard engine and fuselage. I gradually closed in and came dead astern and put another 6 second burst into the port engine. The E/A now went into a steep slide slipping turn to starboard and as we passed almost underneath him Sgt Fletcher put another burst of 1½ seconds into him. Black smoke was pouring out of both engines of E/A which we identified as an HE 111.

All of sudden a lone Luftwaffe night fighter aircraft got on the tail of his aircraft, later recorded in the combat report by the Airgunner.

> Taking evasive action and shook him off twice. But this was not the case, due to the aircraft internal intercom being broken, Sergeant Fletcher was desperately trying to get his pilot attention to take evasive action as an enemy aircraft followed them all the way from Paris over the French coast at 12,000ft. The German aircraft fired off 8 red signal flares at specific intervals of its attacking flight. Unaware of this event, the Intruder safely landed back at RAF Ford early hours of the morning.

> Bombs: 18 x 40lb (G.P) and 60 x 4lb (I.B)
> 1297 rounds of cannon.

Bertie was credited with a 'probable' of a Ju 88, and a 'destroyed' for a He 111 from this engagement. Official Luftwaffe reports state no combat losses occurred at Le Bourget airfield over the night of 3–4 May.

His next recorded skirmish with the enemy was over the night of 7–8 May, again flying Havoc *D-Don*, with Sherrington and Fletcher completing his crew. Taking off from RAF Ford, their mission was to conduct Intruder operations in the vicinity of Villacoublay airfield, Northern France. Bertie

Studio photo as a
Flight Lieutenant
when serving
with 23 Squadron,
1941. (Courtesy of
R. Russell)

took his aircraft low over the target, looking for his intended prey; the engagement is recorded in his combat report:

> The aerodrome was active when we arrived, about 4 E/A circling firing 4 whites and one with navigation and head lights going into land. I was too far away to attack him so decided to do a run over the flare path and drop my bombs as he was landing. I made a diagonal run and dropped a stick of 24 x 40 lbs from 5,000ft. No incendiaries were carried, and no bomb bursts were seen, but the lights of the landing E/A when they reached a point on the runway directly under our A/C, went out and a fire started which burned for about 10–12 minutes. All the aerodrome lights went out and a 4 one-star reds were fired from the ground. From what was seen of the

E/A it appeared that it was either hit by the bombs or that it ran into the crater made by them and caught fire.

Bombs: 24x 40lb (G.P) bombs

Bertie's aircraft was soon in danger from a devious Luftwaffe night fighter aircraft that 'bounced' them from behind; the Havoc took evasive action, and flew low towards the heart of Paris.

> The Black-out was very bad and all details could easily be seen in the bright moonlight. The Eiffel Tower had two bands of red lights round it, one near the top and other half the way down.

Credited with a 'probable' for this action, Bertie landed safely back at RAF Ford. Official Luftwaffe records do not document any loss or damage to any aircraft at Villacoublay airfield over the night of 7–8 May.

An artist's impression of Bertie Hoare, drawn by William Rothenstein in 1941, when serving as a Flight Commander with 23 Squadron when he was based at RAF Ford. Rothenstein was a famous English painter, printer, and draughtsman, and continued to produce art up until his death on 14 February 1945. (Courtesy of RAF Museum, Hendon)

On the night of 11 May, taking off from RAF Ford in Havoc *B-Beer*, Bertie reached the French coast and proceeded to a Luftwaffe airfield close to the Northern French city of Caen. Having already successfully engaged an unknown aircraft, causing significant damage on his initial attack, he prepared to go in for a second attack when the Blenheim's port wing crashed into its intended target. Miraculously, Bertie regained control of his stricken Havoc. As a result of the damage, Bertie decided to head for the safety of home and landed back at RAF Ford; he was credited with a 'damaged' for this engagement. On inspection of his aircraft after landing, he saw the port wing tip had been completely ripped off; the aircraft was assessed as Category 3 damage,

Flying operational since early 1941, Bertie's bravery and gallant flying was recognised by his Commanding Officer, Wing Commander George Heycock, who submitted to the Air Ministry that Bertie be awarded a Distinguished Flying Cross. The award being approved and gazetted in the *London Gazette* on 30 May, the citation read:

> Since January 1941, this officer has carried out many night operational missions. His bombing attacks have been delivered with great skill often in the face of severe opposition from ground defences, and despite the hazardous nature of these sorties, he seldom returns without valuable information. Flight Lieutenant Hoare has destroyed at least two enemy aircraft and certainly damaged others. He has shown great enthusiasm and gallantry throughout.

June was an uneventful month for Bertie, flying only on three occasions due to poor weather. No claims were made apart from two runway beacons which were bombed and destroyed on 16 June. Late on the evening of 24 June, flying Havoc *B-Beer*, his aircraft suffered 'navigational error' combined with strong cross winds on a sortie over Northern France. Not able to locate the designated target at Le-Bourget airfield, Bertie turned his aircraft and headed for home. The Havoc crew reported what they thought this was the Isle of Wight but was actually the German occupied island of Jersey. Another Havoc, *X-X-Ray* on the same sortie also had similar errors, the result of strong cross winds causing it to veer off its planned flight path. This aircraft piloted by Pilot Officer William Thomas, landed at RAF Middle Wallop, Hampshire.

CENTRAL CHANCERY OF
THE ORDERS OF KNIGHTHOOD,
S! JAMES'S PALACE, S.W.1.

17th July, 1941.

Confidential.

Sir,

   The King will hold an Investiture at Buckingham Palace
on Tuesday, the 29th July, 1941, at which your attendance is
requested.

   It is requested that you should be at the Palace not
later than 10.15 o'clock a.m.

DRESS-Service Dress, Morning Dress or Civil Defence Uniform.

   This letter should be produced on entering the Palace,
as no further card of admission will be issued.

   Two tickets for relations or friends to witness the
Investiture may be obtained on application to this Office
and you are requested to state your requirements on the
form enclosed.

   Please complete the enclosed form and return immediately
to the Secretary, Central Chancery of the Orders of
Knighthood, St. James's Palace, London, S.W.1.

            I am, Sir,

            Your obedient Servant,

Squadron Leader Bertie R. O'B. Hoare,
                D.F.C., R.A.F.O.

                              Secretary.

The investiture invitation to Buckingham Palace for the presentation of Bertie's
DFC. (Courtesy of R. Russell)

Havoc I, *F-Freddie*, serial No BD121. Flying low over the English countryside, this aircraft served with 23 Squadron when they were based at RAF Ford. (Courtesy of 12 OCH)

23 Squadron Havoc I, P-Pip, Serial BJ471, nicknamed 'Evelyn', preparing for an Intruder operation from RAF Ford, late 1941. This aircraft was regularly crewed by Pilot Officer Jack Love, Sergeants Malcom Bunting, and Harry Tiby. (Courtesy of Harry Tilby)

Bertie's next claim was on 13 September, flying Havoc *A-Apple*. Taking off from RAF Ford, his target was to patrol Luftwaffe airfields in the vicinity of Melun, in close proximity to Paris. Flying close to the target airfield he noticed a white flashing beacon north of their orbit close to another Luftwaffe airfield. Turning the aircraft to investigate, he observed red flares being fired into the sky and suddenly an unidentified aircraft was seen making its final approach to land with all its lights on.

> I did a run over the aerodrome with the intention of bombing the flarepath as the enemy aircraft landed, but another enemy aircraft was then seen orbiting with its lights on and I gave chase, firing two bursts at it without seeing results.

A further aircraft was spotted, so Bertie quickly turned his Havoc towards the next intended prey, reported as being no more than 40yds from the target. His gunner, Fletcher, fired a three-second burst, the flash of his own machine guns momentarily blinding him; the enemy aircraft instantly extinguished all of its lights.

The Luftwaffe airfield cautiously waited for a brief period of time before assuming that their prowling RAF foe had left the skies above them; they turned on the runway lights and the aircraft began to make their final approach to land. However, Bertie had been patiently waiting above and soon spotted a further aircraft making its approach to land.

> At 800ft altitude and from astern and slightly below at 100yds range I opened fire on his starboard engine where I saw my DE WILDE striking. In all I had six bursts of about 2½ seconds at each engine and his fuselage, in turn and first the port and then the starboard engine belched black smoke and the enemy aircraft fell away to starboard into a vertical dive from 600ft. Nothing further was seen of him.

Setting a course for home, the Havoc landed safely back at RAF Ford, credited with a 'destroyed' of one He 111, and a 'damaged' for a further one He 111. Official Luftwaffe records state a single He 111, H-6, Werk Nummer 4375, from Luftwaffe unit III./KG 40 received 30 per cent damage on landing at Beauvais airfield on this date and at the estimated time that

Bertie's Havoc was in the vicinity of the Luftwaffe airfield. However, there is no mention of a second aircraft being engaged.

On 24 September Bertie was posted to HQ 11 Group, Hillingdon House, RAF Uxbridge, Middlesex; this was only for a short period, conducting staff duties. Nevertheless, he did keep up his operational flying with 23 Squadron, both on 23 October, flying Havoc *T-Toc*, and on 15 November, flying Havoc *J-Johnnie*, as a 'visitor' on Intruder operations. He returned to his squadron permanently on 10 December and was promoted to the temporary rank of Squadron Leader, 'flying' on 1 December, gazetted in the *London Gazette* on 16 December 1941. On 28 December, Bertie piloted a Havoc patrolling over the French city of Lille late at night, but did not locate any targets. He did, however, locate a secondary at the large German marshalling yard close to Bethune in Northern France.

Wing Commander Rupert Leigh, Bertie's Commanding Officer, wrote a letter to him informing him of his short term posting to HQ 11 Group.

11 Group
20 Sept 41

Sammy,

I've bad news for you. The AOC [Air Officer Commanding] sent for me and I've just seen him. The reason for the visit was to tell me that he was going to take you away from me. The job is Night Ops with Peter Townsend at 11 Group. He said he'd been right through all the NF Squadrons and all the S/Ls were rather too young or too inexperienced. And you'd been at the racket sometime. I tried everything on him to dissuade him, but he was adamant. Please note this – this is the first breath of anything of this kind that I have heard, and I'm NOT doing you dirt.

As a small amount of comfort (?), he said that if you behave yourself, (I said you'd loathe it) he might give you a NF squadron in the spring.

One thing I did say when asked if I'd thought you'd do the job well, I said yes but you'd loathe it, and he said it was no good arguing.

In haste, see you on your return.
PHAZ

Above and opposite above: Enjoying a period of leave, this was a rare occasion for Bertie as he flew operational for nearly two years between 1941–42 with little rest. (Courtesy of R. Russell)

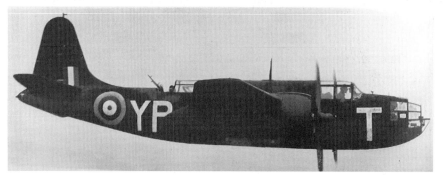

23 Squadron Havoc I inscribed on the reverse of the original photo, 'the famous' *T-Toc*, Serial BD112. Bertie piloted this aircraft on many sorties throughout 1941. It went on to serve at a RAF training unit, finally being used as a ground instructional airframe. (Courtesy of T. Cushing)

OFFICER COMMANDING
23 SQUADRON

1942

The start of 1942 began with poor weather hampering flying operations, with further difficulties of the main runways at RAF Ford still not having been completed. 418 Squadron, Royal Canadian Air Force, who were stationed at RAF Bradwell Bay, Middlesex, were non-operational and this increased the flying tempo for 23 Squadron who had to provide complete coverage for RAF Intruder operations over both Northern France and the Netherlands. To help with this task the squadron split, operating from temporary lodging stations. Half the squadron, under the command of Flight Lieutenant Ken 'Scruffy' Sutton, moved to RAF Manston on 7 January, with the remaining half of the squadron, including HQ elements, moving to RAF Tangmere, West Sussex, on 9 January. Bertie moved with the half that were billeted at RAF Tangmere.

On 28 January, Bertie piloted Havoc *U-Uncle,* taking off from RAF Tangmere en route to Dinard-Pleurtuit airfield, close to the French city of Saint Malo. He was not able to reach the target due to poor weather and successfully landed back at his home airfield. This sortie had Flight Sergeant Albert Gregory fly as Bertie's Air Gunner–Wireless Operator for the first time; he went on to fly most operational sorties on Bertie's crew, both on Havocs and Bostons.

Dinard-Pleurtuit airfield remained a target for the squadron and on 11 February, flying a Boston and taking off from RAF Tangmere, Bertie successfully reached the intended target, having received light flak from ground anti-aircraft positions at Saint Malo and Le-Jouan, a Luftwaffe 'decoy'

Flight Sergeant Albert Gregory, awarded a DFC, gazetted on 13 July 1943, he left the RAF in late 1947 attaining the rank of Flight Lieutenant. (Courtesy of BoB Archive)

airfield. Dinard-Pleurtuit was reported as being active. Bertie flew his Boston low across the airfield and dropped a stick of 4 x 250lb bombs East–West across the runway, observing two of his bombs impact the ground.

On 13 February he was posted on a short-term loan to assist with umpire duties at 10 Group on a Home Defence exercise, returning to operational flying on 27 February. March was an eventful month, with Bertie completing only four operational sorties. On 9 March, piloting a Boston, his aircraft dropped 4 x 250lbs bombs on a German marshalling yard on the outskirts of the French city of Caen. On 26 March, flying a Havoc, his aircraft dropped a payload of 4 x 250lbs bombs against ground targets in the area of Saint Andre, located in the Northern French region of Brittany.

April saw the squadron target priorities remain German marshalling yards, and late on the night of 1 April, Bertie piloted a Boston accompanied by a second, this aircraft was piloted by Flight Lieutenant Kendrick Salusbury-Hughes. Both aircraft dropped bombs on a German marshalling yard at Ameins, Northern France. Bertie's Boston is recorded as releasing a total of 4 x 250lb bombs against its target at 00:25.

Over the night of 2–3 April, Bertie was flying over Northern France looking for potential targets, before arriving in the overhead of Evreux airfield. The Luftwaffe airfield laid quiet with no aircraft activity seen to be landing or taking off. Piloting his lone Intruder to locate further targets, Bertie found a large German industrial factory situated north of the River

Preparing to take off on a sortie in Havoc *R-Robert*. (Courtesy of RAF Historical Branch)

Seine at Mantes Gassicourt, dropping his aircraft's payload of 4 x 250lb bombs on the large structure, resulting in a direct hit.

Bertie took his aircraft back over the Luftwaffe airfield at Evreux, and noticed a number of aircraft preparing to land with their landing lights on. Immediately all these aircraft turned them off. Orbiting the airfield, Bertie closed in on four of them, his air gunners firing their cannons without results. However, he soon closed into what he believed was a Do 215 which had just taken off. Again he ordered his crew to fire at the opportunity target, ranging from 200yds to 70yds from his intended prey. He had to call off the attack when a ground searchlight blinded him in the cockpit. Immediately above him another enemy aircraft was spotted and Bertie gave the order to his crew to fire a three-second burst. This strike hit the intended target, which immediately doused its lights and turned to port; Bertie was credited with two 'damaged' for this engagement.

The Do 215 was not being employed as a bomber at this stage of the war, especially in the West. The Do 17 had been replaced by the Do 217 with specific units from KG 2 and KG 40, both Staffels based in Holland, and forward basing in France. Neither units reported any damage or losses to aircraft over this date.

Further sorties on the 3rd, 10th, and 14th of April were all uneventful due to bad weather and squadron aircraft were unable to locate suitable targets. On the night of 16–17 April, Bertie was patrolling over Montdidier, north of Paris in a Boston; no activity was sighted,

A photograph taken from Bertie's escape documents; he would have to use this identification if he had to bail out over occupied Europe to assist his escape and avoid capture. (Authors Collection)

so he decided to pilot his Boston towards the Luftwaffe base at Beauvais, where he noticed activity on the ground.

Decreasing his aircraft's altitude to get better identification of the enemy airfield, his Boston started to receive heavy flak from the ground defences with five ground searchlights trying to pinpoint his aircraft in the sky. Evading all of these, he noticed a single Luftwaffe aircraft and a number of runway marking lights on the airfield before they were completely turned off. He dropped a total of 12 x 40lb and 2 x 250lb bombs on the intended targets without any confirmed result. Landing back at RAF Ford, Bertie stepped out the cockpit to be given the excellent news that he had been promoted to acting Wing Commander from that date onwards, taking command over the squadron with immediate effect from Wing Commander William Crisham, who was promoted to Group Captain and took command as Station Commander at RAF Kirton in Lindsay, Lincolnshire.

COMMANDING OFFICER
23 SQUADRON

On the night of 25 April, one of Bertie's junior pilots, Pilot Officer Ronald Pegram, was flying on a sortie over Northern France where he dropped a number of bombs – and a little something extra – on a large German industrial factory near the town of Creil. The incident was reported in the squadron log: 'An addition to the usual complement of bombs was an empty Champagne bottle (Ronson Curee de Reserve 1929) presented by W/C Hoare in celebration of assuming command of the squadron.'

Pilot Officer Ronald Desmond Pegram dropped a bottle of Champagne over German targets in Northern France on the 25 April 1942 to celebrate Bertie's promotion to Wing Commander. He was KIA on 31 May 1942 on operations over Breda Airfield, Holland, flying Boston III, serial W8374. His crew, Flight Sergeant T. Rankin was also killed, Sergeant E.W. Nightingale was taken PoW. Pegram was 21 years of age. (Courtesy of P. Stokes)

Air Vice Marshal William Joseph Crisham, was Commanding Officer 23 Squadron, and was succeeded by Bertie on the 17 April 1942. (Courtesy of RAF Museum)

With ongoing station admin and squadron duties Bertie only completed one further sortie that month, on 26 April over Caen. His aircraft released a number of bombs on an Luftwaffe airfield without any confirmed results. Continuing to lead the squadron from the front, Bertie flew a total of five sorties in May. The most significant of these was on 28 May, flying Boston *H-Harry,* taking off from RAF Ford to patrol over German positions in Northern France, focusing on Juvincourt airfield. Reaching the target he noticed an aircraft taxiing along the runway; he turned his aircraft and dropped a total of 18 x 40lb and 1 x 250lb bombs on his target. He observed four bursts impact on the ground and saw the second and third explode immediately in front of the nose of the stricken enemy aircraft. Its navigation lights immediately went out and Bertie and crew assessed it had been destroyed. En route back to RAF Ford, three locomotives were spotted moving at speed south-east of Ameins under the cover of darkness. Descending to 500ft Bertie strafed the locomotive and carriages twice, observing bullets striking the side of the steam engine. His other two victims each received only one pass and again Bertie saw his bullets hit the intended targets before returning and landing safely back at home.

He flew two nights in succession on 30 and 31 May, resulting in limited success. On the first sortie, his aircraft dropped a bomb payload on the edge of an enemy airfield at Deelen, Netherlands. The second, having been diverted due to lack of activity over his primary target, he successfully bombed a marshalling yard at Tergnier, north-east of Paris, followed by a troop transport locomotive which was reported to be struck by the front and rear lower guns of his Havoc.

June was a busy flying period for Bertie. On 8 June he flew as part of a formation of four aircraft, their mission was to attack targets around the Juvincourt area, his aircraft releasing a stick of bombs on the enemy airfield and finishing with a strafe on a single locomotive.

For his enduring combat operations, Bertie was awarded a Bar to his DFC gazetted in the *London Gazette* on 5 June 1942.

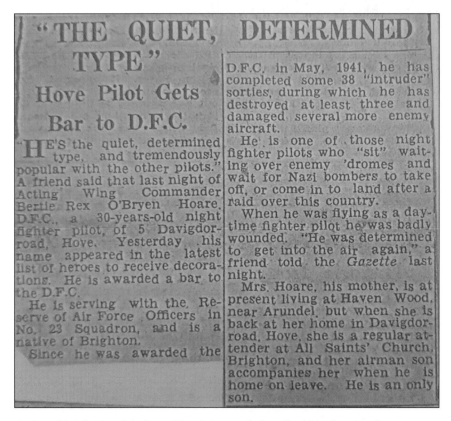

"THE QUIET, DETERMINED TYPE"

Hove Pilot Gets Bar to D.F.C.

"HE'S the quiet, determined type, and tremendously popular with the other pilots." A friend said that last night of Acting Wing Commander Bertie Rex O'Bryen Hoare, D.F.C., a 30-years-old night fighter pilot, of 5 Davigdor-road, Hove. Yesterday his name appeared in the latest list of heroes to receive decorations. He is awarded a bar to the D.F.C.

He is serving with the Reserve of Air Force Officers in No. 23 Squadron, and is a native of Brighton.

Since he was awarded the D.F.C. in May, 1941, he has completed some 38 "intruder" sorties, during which he has destroyed at least three and damaged several more enemy aircraft.

He is one of those night fighter pilots who "sit" waiting over enemy 'dromes and wait for Nazi bombers to take off, or come in to land after a raid over this country.

When he was flying as a daytime fighter pilot he was badly wounded. "He was determined to get into the air again," a friend told the *Gazette* last night.

Mrs. Hoare, his mother, is at present living at Haven Wood, near Arundel, but when she is back at her home in Davigdor-road, Hove, she is a regular attender at All Saints' Church, Brighton, and her airman son accompanies her when he is home on leave. He is an only son.

A close friend, when hearing of Bertie's award, described him in a local newspaper, the *Sussex Daily News*. 'He's the quiet, determined type, and tremendously popular with the other pilots'. (Courtesy of R. Russell)

Since being awarded the Distinguished Flying Cross in May 1941, this officer has completed some 38 Intruder sorties during which he has destroyed at least 3 and damaged several more enemy aircraft. He has at all times set an inspiring example.

On 7 June, 23 Squadron received delivery of a single Mosquito TIII aircraft to conduct conversion to this type of aircraft, and eventually replacing their ageing Havocs and Bostons with the Mosquito NF Mk II. A total of twenty-five Mark II aircraft was especially produced under contract number 555/C.23(a) at the Hatfield factory, Hertfordshire. Approved on 9 February 1941, these airframes were devoid of an airborne interception radar, which at the time were considered too valuable to risk falling into enemy hands.

On 12 June, Bertie received an unusual letter from the Medical Officer who had treated him for his eye injury at RAF Henlow two years earlier, congratulating him on his Bar to his DFC.

CME/OP1/23/59
Ophthalmic Department
Centre Medical Establishment
Awdry House, Kingsway W.C
12 June 1942

Dear Hoare,
May I congratulate you heartily upon your peculiar and highly effective habits in the night sky.

It was a very good wind which blew me into Pattison's office and allowed time to think upon your eye condition with night flying. I am perfectly convinced that your very dilated pupil with a healthy eye behind it is of assistance in allowing you to pick up objects with this high degree of success.

In view of the fact that I have tried this method artificially, and considered then that it was most promising, I am all the more glad to see that part of the argument has been proved by yourself from another angle.

Mosquito N.F II DD670, YP-S. (Courtesy of markstyling.com)

As squadron commanding officer, Bertie was the first to fly Mosquito *S-Sugar* on the evening of 5 July. Taking off from RAF Ford with his Observer, Pilot Officer Sydney Corness, he flew low over the French city of Caen but no activity was sighted. They did, however, experience heavy flak over Le Havre before returning safely back to RAF Ford.

Bertie had further success on the early hours of the morning of 6–7 July, again flying Mosquito *S-Sugar*, this time with Warrant Officer John Potter as his Observer. The following is an extract from Bertie's combat report for this engagement:

> I took off from Ford with W/O Potter, at 00:10 to patrol Avord. As we approached Chartres we saw a cone of about 10 searchlights up over the aerodrome. These doused, then came on again, then doused and came on vertically upwards. Then they doused. Immediately afterwards, Potter saw an e/a with navigation lights coming on towards us from the direction of Chartres at the same height as us, 2,000ft. I did a wide orbit and stalked the e/a, approaching from astern and 200–300ft below. As we approached we suddenly realised we were much nearer to the E/A than we thought, I throttled back but could not avoid overshooting slightly. I turned away to the side and made another approach. As I turned away I recognised it as a Do.217. I opened fire with cannons only from astern and slightly below at about 100yds and the first burst set the starboard engine on fire. I gave two bursts and the fuselage

caught fire. During the last burst there was a dull thud on the windscreen, and from the mess it left it is thought to have been a 'piece' of the rear gunner. I broke off the attack and the E/A which was burning furiously, glided down and crashed just short of the aerodrome, whose lights had come on, when the e/a flashed his head light just before my attack. Just after the E/A hit the ground there was a large explosion and it remained burning on the ground until we were out of sight on our way to AVORD. There was no apparent activity at Avord, so we set a course for base and landed at 03:10.

Official Luftwaffe reports state a single aircraft crashed sixteen miles east of Chartres airfield. This engagement saw the first official claim against an enemy aircraft by a 23 Squadron Mosquito since they had been brought into service. Bertie was promoted to the substantive rank of Squadron Leader on 17 July, gazetted in *the London Gazette* on 2 October 1942.

Late on the evening of 30 July, flying an unrecorded Mosquito with Corness as his Observer, they were patrolling over the Luftwaffe airfield at Orleans-Bricy, south-west of Paris. The following is taken from the combat report for this engagement:

I took off from Ford at 00:10 to patrol over Orleans. On arrival there, all the aerodrome lights and Visual Lorenz were on. We orbited for about half an hour during which time they were all switched off and on several times. At about 01:30 hours an aircraft landed before I was able to attack as he only put his lights on at about 200ft and all lights was immediately extinguished when he landed. It was a very light night, so I orbited very low and close to see if I could see him taxiing to his dispersal. As I was doing this, the aerodrome lights came on and a red light was seen to move out towards No.1 flare. I thought this was an E/A taxying out and preparing to attack it when an E/A came into land putting his navigation and headlight at about 200ft. I immediately climbed up to 1,500ft, turned and attacked from stern as he was touching down. I opened fire with cannon only, at about 1,000ft with a long, followed by a short burst, many strikes were seen and the E/A (unidentified twin engine), caught fire and burned furiously. As I was diving to attack, a Bofors type gun opened up from the position of the red light that I had seen move out to No.1 flare. This flak was very close.

Due to loss of the VHF radio communications in his aircraft, Bertie landed at RAF Exeter, Devon, in the early hours of the morning. The Luftwaffe aircraft that was destroyed was recorded as a Focke Wulf 200 Condor, C-3, 0030 coded SG+KF, from IV./KG 40, crewed by Oberleutnant Hermann Frenzel and Unteroffizier Paul Boller, both aircrew were badly injured in this incident.

During August, Bertie flew only a single sortie, over the night of 1–2 August, with his Observer, Corness; flying Mosquito *B-Beer*, he stalked targets above enemy airfields situated around Chartres and Orleans, Northern France. At Evreux airfield they observed three small fires and several landing lights, so Bertie took his aircraft low to investigate. Suddenly searchlights came on, throwing beams of light into the sky from

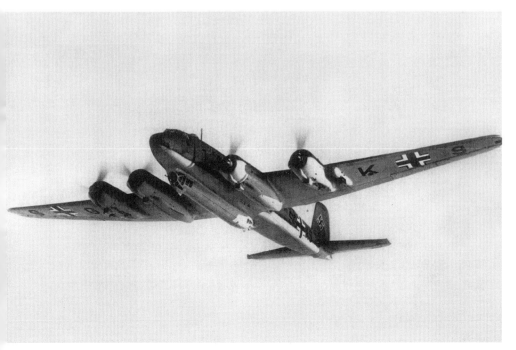

A Fw200 C-3, coded SG+KS, of IV./KG 40, a similar aircraft to the one shot down over the night 30 and 31 July. (Courtesy of Asisbiz.com)

Pilot Officer Sydney Corness was chosen by Bertie to be his Observer, pictured here between July and December 1942. He was lost on operations serving with 23 squadron over Tunis on 21 February 1943. (Courtesy of P. Corness)

ground defences that heard the distinctive sound of the Mosquito's engines, combined with heavy flak which was close to his aircraft. Bertie decided to not loiter and so headed for home, landing back at RAF Ford. After a series of uneventful sorties at the beginning of September, Bertie's next claim was on 10 September, flying over an enemy airfield close to the city of Enschede, Netherlands. Flying Mosquito *B-Beer*, with Potter as his Observer, they reached the Dutch coastline at 21:46. The following is taken from the squadron report on completion of this sortie:

> Twente / Enschede was reached at 22:25 hours, but, as the aerodrome was not lit, the Mosquito carried on course for a few minutes, and saw the aerodrome at Hopsten lit with a fairly bright flarepath and a dim Visual Lorenz both running E to W. There was a rotating beacon at the east end of the Visual Lorenz. These lights stayed on throughout the patrol. At 22:40 hours, when the Mosquito was about 12 miles NE of Twente Enschede the E-W Visual Lorenz and flarepath there seem to come on and the Mosquito flew towards it.

Getting within four miles of the flarepath and peering into the darkness attempting to make out any target aircraft, a light was spotted moving slowly in the sky at around 1,500ft, travelling west down towards the Lorenz beacon. Giving chase, Bertie manoeuvred his aircraft behind his target.

> The e/a with a very bright white-orange light in its tail turned left and had we followed straight after it, we would have gone across the middle of the aerodrome. We therefore skirted the aerodrome and continued the chase.

Alerted by the looming Intruder, the enemy aircraft picked up its speed and went into a shallow dive; it was not able to outrun the speed of the Mosquito, which caught up with its prey at 400ft, firing its awesome array of cannons against the stricken bomber.

> I turned off as the light was far too bright to make a stern attack upon it. The e/a appeared to slow down, we overshot and did a complete orbit as the e/a hit the ground and burst into flames, scattering burning pieces circled it.

'Hide and Seek', a painting depicting 23 Squadron N.F II Mosquito, R-Ron, serial DD797 on an Intruder sortie, having just downed a German He 111. R-Ron was lost in a flying accident on 26 November 1942 Crewed by Sergeant Duncan Stuart Hutt, RCAF and his Observer, Sergeant Gurwyn Malcom Cridge, RAFVR, it took off from RAF Bradwell Bay on a training flight and crashed at West Mersea, Essex. Both were crew were killed in the crash. Bertie piloted this aircraft on 24 September on an Intruder sortie to Beauvais and Creil, Northern France. (Painter unknown)

Bertie was credited with a 'destroyed' for this engagement. Luftwaffe records state no losses at this time from combat or flying accidents at Twente airfield.

On the night of 13–14 September again flying over Twente, Netherlands. Flying *B-Beer* with Potter flying as his Observer, their aircraft was hit by ground fire at Haamstede, Netherlands. The starboard engine had been completely destroyed by flak damage, and using his skill and experience Bertie limped home the stricken '*Mossy*' on only one engine, which was also not functioning correctly. On reaching the English coast they were guided to safety by friendly marker searchlights where Bertie carried out a forced landing at RAF Hunsdon, Essex, at 03:10. Both crew were lucky and walked away from the incident.

COMMANDING OFFICER 23 SQUADRON

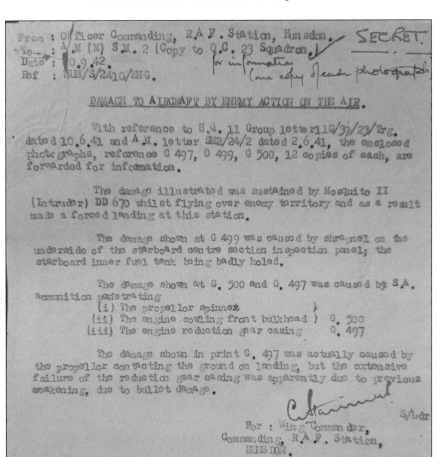

From : Officer Commanding, R.A.F. Station, Hunsdon.   SECRET.
To.. : A.M (M) S.M. 2 (Copy to O.C. 23 Squadron.)
Date : 10.9.42.   for information
Ref : HUN/S/2410/ENG.   (one copy of each photograph)

DAMAGE TO AIRCRAFT BY ENEMY ACTION ON THE AIR.

With reference to H.Q. 11 Group letter 11G/39/23/Trg.
dated 10.6.41 and A.M. letter SM2/24/2 dated 2.6.41, the enclosed
photographs, reference G 497, G 499, G 500, 12 copies of each, are
forwarded for information.

The damage illustrated was sustained by Mosquito II
(Intruder) DD 670 whilst flying over enemy territory and as a result
made a forced landing at this station.

The damage shown at G 499 was caused by shrapnel on the
underside of the starboard centre section inspection panel; the
starboard inner fuel tank being badly holed.

The damage shown at G. 500 and G. 497 was caused by S.A.
ammunition penetrating
        (i) The propellor spinner   )
        (ii) The engine cowling front bulkhead) G. 500
        (iii) The engine reduction gear casing   G. 497

The damage shown in print G. 497 was actually caused by
the propellor contacting the ground on landing, but the extensive
failure of the reduction gear casing was apparently due to previous
weakening, due to bullet damage.

                                                    S/Ldr
                        For : Wing Commander,
                    Commanding, R.A.F. Station,
                    HUNSDON.

Above, right and overleaf: An official RAF report and photos showing the damage to Mosquito *B-Beer* DD670 that Bertie was piloting when he had to carry out a force landing at RAF Hunsdon early on the morning of 14 September 1942 due to flak damage. (Courtesy of E. Eyre)

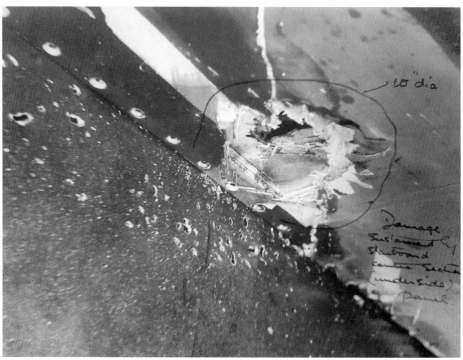

Finally rested from operational flying on 24 September, Bertie reluctantly handed over his squadron command to Wing Commander Peter Wykeham-Barnes, having completed a total of exactly eighty Intruder sorties with his time serving with 23 squadron. The squadron log recorded:

> He goes into what is hoped will be only temporary retirement from 'Intruder' operations with a score of six enemy aircraft destroyed, four probably destroyed and four damaged. Now he is to train more 'cats' eyes' pilots in a game which is anything but quiet.

The day after departing the squadron Bertie was awarded the Distinguished Service Order for exemplary service and command, gazetted in the *London Gazette* on 9 October 1942.

> This officer has completed numerous operational sorties over enemy occupied territory during which he has destroyed six enemy aircraft. Since Wing Commander Hoare assumed command, the squadron has destroyed at least seven enemy aircraft, and damaged others, a result reflecting the greatest credit on this officer's excellent leadership. He has inspired confidence in those under his command.

Air Marshal Sir Lawrence Arthur Pattinson wrote a letter to Bertie congratulating him on his award of the DSO.

UNITED UNIVERSITY CLUB
1, SUFFOLK STREET, S.W.1
12/10/42

Dear Rex,
I have just heard from my wife that the DSO has been awarded to your other glories and I write to send you my very hearty congratulations, you must have put up a great show and I am delighted that you have succeeded in making such a good impression on the enemy without being shot down on the many rides or even wounded.

I have returned to the service as AVM, and I am going out to one of our allies at a very great distance and for an indefinite time as head of a small RAF mission. Most certainly connected with keeping their staff college. In the meantime, I am in the Air Ministry for 3 weeks or so longer, trying to sort out the information that I shall need for the job + being vaccinated against every sort of disease. I am as you can imagine very pleased to be back.

Don't bother to answer this. Best of luck to you in your new command.

Yours ever
L.A. Pattison

Above left: Air Marshal Peter Guy Wykeham, at the rank of Wing Commander assumed command of 23 Squadron on 23 September 1942. (Courtesy of IWM)

Above right: Bertie with Tadzee displaying his epic sized handlebar moustache, this photo was posed for *War Illustrated* magazine, 11 December 1942, issue 143. (Courtesy of T. Cushing)

60 OPERATIONAL TRAINING UNIT

1943

60 Operational Training Unit was formed on 28 April 1941 under the command of No 81 Group, based at RAF Leconfield, East Riding. Initially flying Blenheims and Defiant aircraft, teaching pilots and their crews the art of night fighting in the air. The unit was disbanded on 24 November 1942, with all its personnel and stores being transferred between No 132 OTU and No 51 OTU. The latter received No 2 Squadron, (Night Intruder) based at RAF Twinwood Farm, Bedfordshire, where Bertie was a senior flying Instructor. The unit's primary role was to train seven Intruder crews per month; however, this training cycle was increased to sixteen crews per month. On 17 May, 60 OTU was reformed as a half OTU, under the direct command of Bertie; the new unit would be based at RAF High Ercall, Shropshire. Bertie had arrived early, on 15 May, and the unit received full operating training status on 2 July; Bertie recalled, 'forming 60 OTU was a tricky business'. Often visiting RAF colleagues at various commands and asking if they wished to join his elite band of night fighter pilots. Flying Officers Hector Goldie and Norman Conquer remembering such a visit.

> Early in June we were visited at Bicester by none other than Sammy Hoare, Wing Commander Flying, and Chief Instructor of a new OTU, No 60 at High Ercall, Shropshire, being set up to train pilots for intruder missions, flying not the Blenheim, but Mosquitos. We attend the course between June – September.

No 1 Course, 60 OTU, RAF High Ercall, 1943. (Courtesy of Aircrew Remembered)

A tragic flying accident occurred at RAF High Ercall on 13 August 1943, involving an instructor pilot, Flying Officer Peter Stokes who was an experienced and knowledgeable Mosquito pilot with over 660 flying hours against twenty different aircraft types. He had also served under Bertie's command with 23 Squadron prior to being posted as an instructor at both 51 and 60 OTU. That evening he was piloting Mosquito NF MkII, serial No DD630, taking off at 20:50 from RAF High Ercall to complete a test flight, prior to the aircraft being used later that evening by a student pilot and himself as the instructor. What was not known, however, is that he had a passenger onboard – his civilian wife, Daphne Stokes. The following extract is taken from the official RAF crash investigation report:

> Precis of Investigation No. W1616
> F/O Stokes took off at approximately 20:50, on August 13th to carry out a routine night flying test on this aircraft which it had been arranged that he should use later the same evening. Shortly after take-off he was seen to carry out at least one low dive across the airfield and after an interval he came back across the airfield from east to west. When approaching the airfield boundary, he completed one roll which is described as being perfectly executed, although it was neither a slow barrel

roll or a flick roll, but something between the two completed on a more or less horizontal line without loss of height. After a very brief pause he began a second similar roll but the initial speed appeared to be lower and when he was approximately inverted it seems probable that the engines cut (which would be quite normal), the aircraft lost speed and completed the roll in a stalled condition. At this point there seems to have been a burst of flame from the port engine, and while witnesses differ as to the exact moment at which this was seen and its duration, there is little doubt that it was due to the upsetting of the mixture by the attitude of the aircraft as the engine cut in again and that the aircraft was not actually on fire on its way down. As the aircraft completed the second roll it appears to have flicked over into a spin from a height of less than 1,000ft, and after completing little more than one turn it struck the ground on the tarmac runway and burst into flames. Both occupants were killed. The question of the unauthorised carrying of Mrs Stokes as passenger was fully considered by the Service Court of Inquiry and does not enter into this investigation.

As the spin commenced two pieces were seen to leave the aircraft and they were subsequently identified as the rear entry door and a right hand undercarriage door, but whether from the port or starboard side is not known. The wreckage covered only a small area about 50yds in diameter apart from the two pieces already referred to which fell within the airfield boundary, but as the runway was required for night flying that night the wreckage was moved some 80 to 100yds on to the grass and on the instructions of the AOC was transferred to 34 M.U. of Shrewsbury the following day just before the Inspector of Accidents arrived.

The aircraft was so completely destroyed by impact and fire followed by the subsequent double removal before it could be examined that little useful information could be obtained. It was however apparent that there had been no major structural failure before impact and that all control surfaces were in position. There is no suggestion by any witness that the manoeuvres carried out were other than intentional or that the two parts which became detached did so before the very severe final flick stall.

The Station Engineering Officer at High Ercall had retained those parts of the undercarriage which could be identified and it is clear from the condition of the latches attached to the oleo legs in conjunction with the eyewitnesses' statements that neither half of the undercarriage came down. It was possible to say from the condition of those parts of the tail end which remained and from the state of the undercarriage and rear entry door which became detached that there was no possibility of these parts being struck in the air in such a way as to interfere with control.

It was considered that this incident was due solely to loss of flying speed in the course of aerobatics carried out at too low a height to allow any possibility of recovery from the resulting spin. The two parts which fell separately appear from the evidence of eyewitnesses to have become detached in the course of a sharp flick stall following two rolls probably as the result of unusual air loading in the course of these manoeuvres. They are not held to have any bearing on the accident.

27 August 1943
For C.I (Accidents)

Mr Alf Harris, a civilian Foreman based with a RAF Maintenance unit at RAF High Ercall recalls the incident:

This particular fellow, they had a baby, and his wife came down to stay with him for a few days. If you come up from the Milk Marketing Board place at Crudgington, the first gate you come to, that side of the airfield was the Operational Training Unit where the Mosquitos were based. This fellow got a lady who lived in one of the houses on the road there, near the main gate, to put his wife up and she used to look after the baby for them if they wanted to go out. On the other side of the airfield was 29 Maintenance Unit. She wanted to see what it was like flying a Mosquito. Of course, first they had to get her into the airfield, and then near a plane. They waited until the Friday morning, and kitted her out with the uniform and flying kit, and smuggled her into the airfield, she wouldn't have been allowed to go in. Then off they went. I was not there the actual day. But when I came in on Monday morning there was a big heap of ashes and everything at the crossroads of the runway. This plane, some of the lads that worked with me said, dived down across the airfield and as it pulled up it leaned over as if it was going to do a barrel roll and dived straight into the airfield. They were both killed. Nobody said anything about it. There were not that many people who knew about it. Those that did, it was all whispers as we were told not to say anything about it. It should not have happened. She should not have been allowed on the airfield.

Daphne Joan Stokes was 20 years old when she was killed. She had been married previously to Pilot Officer Ronald Pegram, a fellow pilot of both Peter and Bertie when all three were flying with 23 squadron in 1942. Pegram was lost on operations on 31 May 1942. (Courtesy of P. Stokes)

Both Peter and Daphne were buried together at Wellington General Cemetery, Shropshire. Their son Peter, born on 25 March, recalled, 'I was brought with my mother to RAF High Ercall to meet my father for the very first time.'

Bertie, who was a stickler for rules and regulations, was both angry and deeply saddened with the loss of a close friend and an unnecessary death of a civilian at his airfield.

Flying Officer Peter William Stokes, DFC, he was 22 years old when he was killed. (Courtesy of P. Stokes)

Peter and Daphne on their wedding day. (Courtesy of P. Stokes)

An aerial photograph of RAF High Ercall. From 1942 the US 8th Army Air Force 309th Fighter Squadron was based here, flying Spitfires with USAAF markings. (Author's Collection)

HANDING OVER CERTIFICATE

(a) I hereby certify that I have this day taken over the command of Royal Air Force Station, High Ercall.

(b) I have counted and verified in the manner prescribed in King's Regulations and Air Council Instructions (see para.71, clause 1(e), (f) and (g), all balances of money in the accountant officer's charge, both that in hand at the bank, including public money, airmen's messing account monies and monies held for safe custody, and am satisfied that all cash accounts relating thereto are correct and in order.

(c) I am also satisfied that as far as I am able to ascertain, the stocks and stores (R.A.F. equipment and supplies) and the accounts relating thereto are in order (see A.P.830, Vol.1 Chapter 12) with the exception of those detailed in the annexed list.

(d) I have checked the balances of cash in hand and at the bank, (including investments) of all non-public funds of my command as detailed below and have certified to that effect in the cash accounts of these funds. After examining the books of account and the last balance sheet, I find that these accounts are satisfactory and are not in arrear.

    (i)   Officers' Mess
    (ii) Sergeants' Mess
    (iii) Station Institute
    (iv) C. of E. Church Account
    (v)   National Savings Group

(e) I hereby certify that all secret and confidential publications have been checked in accordance with King's Regulations and Air Council Instructions, para.2243.

...................................Signature as taking over command of Royal Air Force Station, High Ercall.

Certified that I have this day handed over the command of Royal Air Force Station, High Ercall, and have brought to the notice of the Commanding Officer all outstanding correspondence and other matters concerning the command of which he should be informed

...................................Signature. as having handed over the command of Royal Air Force Station, High Ercall.

        Royal Air Force Station,
        High Ercall, Nr. Wellington. Salop.

An official RAF document confirming official handover of RAF High Ercall to Bertie's command. (Courtesy of RAF Historical Branch)

Writing in a letter home he explained he was tired of running a non-operational unit and was keen to get back to a frontline squadron.

Twinwood Farm
Bedfordshire

Dearest Ma,

Many thanks for your letter. Perhaps you are right my mind is out of normal, certainly something is wrong with me. I think it must be the inactivity of this place. But as you are aware my time is now over, and I shall expect to be moving into more exciting things very soon.

I have found the letters you sent me a long time ago, I really must make an effort to write something soon but at the moment I really can't, I don't even see the point writing in our officers' mess now. I really must get myself together, get down to it.

Bye bye, all love as ever
Rex

HQ Flight, RAF Twinwood Farm, January 1943, Bertie seated centre front row with Tadzee the dog. Flying Officer John Potter is middle row, first on the left. (Courtesy of R. Russell)

COMMANDING OFFICER
605 SQUADRON

Taking command of 605 (*County of Warwick*) Royal Air Force Auxiliary Squadron on 25 September 1943, relieving Wing Commander Charles Tomalin. Tomalin's pre-war diving history saw him a member of the Great Britain diving team in 1936 and later becoming team manager at the 1948 Olympic games. Tomalin was treated to a diving display by the RAF swimming gala as a leaving present.

605 Squadron was stationed at RAF Castle Camps, Cambridgeshire, moving to RAF Bradwell Bay, Essex on 6 October, before finally moving to RAF Manston on 7 April 1944. The squadron had transitioned to Mk.VI Mosquitos in February of that year. Squadron aircraft were operating at night in an environment where searchlights were a real danger and the traditional matte black finish that was originally added to the aircraft was found to be less helpful in concealment at

A newspaper article, dated 26 September 1943 confirming Bertie's new posting as Commanding Officer 605 County of Warwick Squadron. (Courtesy of RAF Historical Branch)

Intruder Pioneer Comes Back

Wing-Commander B. R. O'B. Hoare

WING-COMMDR. B. R. O'B. HOARE, DSO, DFC and Bar, one of the pioneers of night intruding over enemy airfields, has returned to operational flying after twelve months training new crews for this type of operation.

He has been posted to command the County of Warwick Squadron, one of the leading intruder squadrons in Fighter Command.

Born at Brighton in 1912, Wing-Commander Hoare has been in the RAF for seven years. In the winter of 1940-41 he was a flight lieutenant in the Blenheim Squadron, which initiated intruder patrols over German bomber bases in Northern France at a time when the Luftwaffe was making its heaviest night attacks on Britain.

When he left the squadron, last autumn, Wing-Commander Hoare had destroyed at least six enemy aircraft.

night. It was decided to repaint them in an overall grey with green disruptive camouflage. However, many aircraft kept their matte black bottom surfaces, even after adding the grey-green uppers.

605 Royal Auxiliary Squadron was formed on 5 October 1926 under orders of Lord Trenchard, Marshal of the Royal Air Force. The Auxiliary Air Force was seen as a corps d'elite composed of the kind of young men who earlier would have been interested in horses, but now wished to serve their country in machines. Trenchard conceived that the new mechanical yeomanry with aeroplanes would be based on the great centres of industry. The original provision was for six Auxiliary squadrons and seven Special Reserve squadrons. Trenchard stressed that this new Auxiliary Air Force was not a 'reserve' for the Royal Air Force but a separate air force altogether, whose role was to be that of day bombers.

On taking command of the squadron, Bertie's first task was to write to the Air Ministry, and specifically Group Captain Lord Willoughby de Broke, who was Deputy Director of Public Relations, informing him of the change of command and to ask his personal thoughts on what the squadron should do to mark the upcoming tally for the squadron.

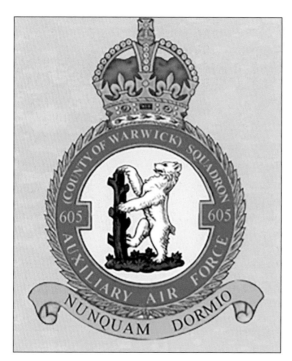

605 'County of Warwick' Squadron, RAF crest, whose motto was, *Nunquam Dormio*, 'I Never Sleep' (Courtesy of RAF Copyright)

I think I am exceedingly lucky to have command of 605 and a better Squadron it would be hard to find and very soon I hope we shall be celebrating the destruction of our hundredth Hun. I don't know if you have any ideas as to what form the celebration should take, but I thought a party for all ranks here as well as a sweepstake, the prize money to be divided between the air crew and ground crew who shoot down the 100th Hun and the winner of the ticket.

Late on the evening of 23 September, with excitement, Bertie took off on his first combat sortie since leaving 23 Squadron over a year before. He was joined with his faithful Observer. Now commissioned, Flying Officer John Potter had specifically been posted to the squadron on Bertie's request. Flying Mosquito *E-Easy,* they patrolled over Luftwaffe airfields in Northern France, no enemy activity was sighted and they returned home.

On the 27 September, flying with Potter in Mosquito *L-Love,* their mission was to patrol enemy airfields North of Hannover, in the heartland

Group Captain Lord Willoughby de Broke was the Deputy Director of Public Relations at the Air Ministry (1941–44) and Director from 1945–46. (Courtesy of the RAFBF)

of Germany. They reached the target area at 22:22 at an altitude of 2,500ft. All was quiet until 23:05 when the Luftwaffe airfield at Dedelsdorf turned on its runway lights. Bertie took this as an indicator that aircraft were preparing to land. The following is taken from the combat report for this sortie:

> At 23:10, two E/A were seen with Navigation lights, one of which was chased without success. We turned our attention to the second and chased it in its circuit from NW to the E end, where he made a very tight turn as if attempting to land. Probably finding this impossible he went around again, was again chased, and again made a tight turn. As he did so I gave him a two second burst of cannon only using 3 to 4 rings of deflection from 300yds, range at 1,000ft, but we saw no results and the E/A landed. We continued our patrol and attacked from astern slightly below from 150yds range at 1,500ft, with two bursts of one to two seconds of cannon only, closing to 70yds. We saw the starboard engine catch fire, identifying it as a DO217, and it crashed just SE of the F.P. where it exploded. The flames from the burning engine were bright enough for F/O Potter, DFC, Observer, to see AI aerials on or just under the nose and the camouflage was similar to that of a night Mosquito.

605 Squadron recorded a large tally for this combat action. Crews Sergeant Henry Collins and Sergeant Douglas Norton destroyed two enemy aircraft over Vechta, near Bremen, Germany. Squadron Leader Thomas Heath and Flying Officer Owain Richards destroyed a further Do 217 over Parchim, eighty miles south-west of Berlin, Germany.

Official Luftwaffe records show multiple losses happened on this date and it is difficult to state exactly which targets were engaged during Bertie's combat. However, it was most likely Bf110 G-4, Werk Nummer 5350, coded G9+EN of 5./NJG, crewed by Hauptmann Hans Werner Rupprecht and Franz Vornhusen, which crashed 1km west of Abbensen, Central Germany, both crew were killed from this combat engagement. The next day a 'special order of the day' was written by Bertie to all members of the squadron.

Congratulations to all ranks on last night's magnificent effort in destroying four Huns. It is not only to the Pilot who presses the trigger, or to the Observer who gets the Pilot to the target, that this success is due, but to each and every member of the Squadron, be he fitter or rigger, clerk or armourer, cook or driver, or one of the many other trades, RAF or WAAF, for without their loyalty, perseverance and hard work, often under difficult and trying conditions, this success could not be won. I am greatly honoured, proud, and happy, to command this redoubtable squadron, and I can only now adjure you all to continue with the same steadfastness of purpose, and I feel sure that last night's wondrous success will not be an isolated, but a regular occurrence.

B.R.O'B. Hoare

October was described in the squadron log as a 'lean' month, with RAF Castle Camps attacked and bombed by the Luftwaffe on the night of the

A Bf110-G variant, similar to the type that Bertie destroyed on the night of 27–28 September 1943, crewed by Hauptmann Hans Werner Rupprecht, and Unteroffizier Franz Vornhusen of 5./NJG. (Courtesy of 12 OCH)

L–R Flying Officer John Frederick Potter and Bertie with Tadzee his dog seated in the middle. Potter served with 214 and 148 Squadron as a Sergeant rank in 1940–41. He was awarded a DFC, gazetted on 30 October 1942 while serving with 23 Squadron. (Courtesy of R. Russell)

2 October. The only person injured was a WAAF driver, named Audrey. She had been blasted out of the hut she was in and was only found several hours later in a field by a searchlight crew going off duty. Thankfully, despite suffering severe bruising and sustaining some damage to her lungs, she was alive and was rushed to Addenbrooke's Hospital, Cambridge. This event was recorded in the squadron log:

> A WAAF driver belonging to the flarepath party was blown 10ft in the air out of her bed when a bomb hit the end of her hut and 'B' Flight were a bit damaged. But were very lucky in that a can of Butterflys which landed 10yds outside the hut did not go off.

While this attack was unfolding over RAF Castle Camps, Bertie and Potter were flying in Mosquito *L-Love* patrolling above a Luftwaffe airfield at Laupheim, Southern Germany, with little activity observed. On landing back at home, they were shocked to hear of the Luftwaffe attack on their airfield.

On 5 October, Bertie broke the news to the squadron they were moving to RAF Bradwell Bay, Essex, recorded in the squadron log:

> We were loath to leave FORD but we have settled in very comfortably and wonder if we shall be as comfortable at our new base. There is no question that in our new squadron mess at CASTLE CAMPS, where we have everything to ourselves we have been very happy. But shall no doubt settle in quickly become 'acclimatised' in short term.

The Station Commander of RAF Ford was not sorry to see the back of 605 who were last seen chasing a 3-ton truck driven by Corporal Norman Wilkinson, which was allegedly spiriting away some of his precious cotton bed sheets, while bidding a fond farewell with the sentiment: 'Get off my station, you 605 lot would roll up the runway if you could.'

The Station Commander of RAF Bradwell Bay was Wing Commander Russell Aitken, and as reported in the squadron log: 'He is very Intruder "minded" as he was an Intruder Controller at 11 Group for some time when 605 were forming at FORD, he has done all in his power to make us at home.' The squadron were given only one day to settle into their new home and reported at full operational readiness by 7 October, with Intruder missions being flown over targets in occupied Belgium that night.

One of these aircraft was *L-Love*, with Bertie and Potter flying low over the Belgium coastline at 2,500ft; they reached the target area of Le Culot at 22:20, with low cloud hindering visibility. The Mosquito descended to 1,000ft and headed towards the main Luftwaffe airfield at Brussels. This airfield was seen to be active at 22:11 with the runway reported as being marked by a single line of flares. The lone Intruder waited quietly above the Luftwaffe airfield for any unsuspecting prey. At 22:45 a single unidentified aircraft was seen to land left of the flare path, too late to engage, a second was observed at 23:14, which approached the runway with its landing lights on. Bertie manoeuvred his aircraft south-east of the target area, here he pushed his throttle and stick forward and at 1,500ft dived towards his foe. Attacking this from the starboard quarter, he fired a short cannon burst. Cannon strikes were observed going across the flight path of the descending aircraft, immediately a searchlight was turned on from the airfield defences that went searching for the attacking Intruder, which departed at 23:42.

Wing Commander Russell Faulkner Aitken, AFC nicknamed 'Digger', was a native New Zealander, he was the Station Commander at RAF Bradwell Bay in 1943 when 605 Squadron were stationed here. It was reported he was in charge of 3,065 service personnel, ranging from ground echelon to aircrew. He was recorded in RAF history as the youngest Station Commander when he took charge of RAF Hawkinge in September 1942 at the age of 29 years old.. (Courtesy of RAF Commands)

Over the night of 8–9 October, Bertie again flew Mosquito *L-Love* and at 02:43, having successfully reached the target over a Luftwaffe airfield at Dedelsdorf, Germany, his aircraft tipped in to engage the airfield watch office and a single enemy aircraft that was seen taxiing. The Mosquito struck with its formidable 20-inch Hispano cannons and 303-inch Browning machine guns from its nose; the ground defences immediately returned fire, with its light anti-aircraft guns and searchlights scouring the sky looking for the lone Intruder. Evading these lights, the Mosquito sneaked its way back home with a faint glow where the target aircraft was last seen on the taxi way.

Poor weather and training sorties limited operational flying for the squadron until 15 October, with Bertie's next sortie on 20 October patrolling over Luftwaffe airfields in the vicinity of Bergen, Northern Germany, where little activity was sighted; he returned home in the early hours of the next morning.

On 22 October, Bertie had to deal with the loss of one of his crews; not in combat, which he could only just accept, but from a tragic accident. At 03:41, Sergeant Robert Jean Baptiste Edmond Stenuit, a Belgium pilot and his Observer, Flight Sergeant John Finlay McEwen, RCAF, flying Mosquito *Q-Queen,* serial HJ768, hit low trees close to the edge of the runway and exploded instantly, killing both crew members.

Some humour was brought back to squadron life that evening when Flying Officer Bob Muir, the squadron assistant Navigation officer, was preparing to fly on an Intruder sortie with his pilot, Squadron Leader Thomas Heath. Muir was reported to 'distinguish' himself when he fell into a deep water-filled ditch on the airfield, rising from the hole with all his maps and charts drenched. Their mission was cancelled when the R/T plugs failed in the aircraft, which was believed to be from damp, reported as 'a result of his bath!'

The squadron excelled on flying operational sorties over 22 October in appalling weather conditions; their achievement was recognised and praise was given to the squadron by AOC, Air Chief Marshal Sir Trafford Leigh-Mallory.

> The number of sorties flown against the enemy last night under appalling weather conditions reflects the greatest credit on all concerned. My heartiest congratulations. Leigh Mallory.

Flight Sergeant John Finlay McEwen, RCAF, was killed with his pilot, Sergeant Robert Jean Baptiste Edmond STENUIT, 'Belgium', on the morning of 22 October 1943, taking off from RAF Bradwell Bay in Mosquito *Q-Queen,* serial HJ768, to conduct Intruder operations over Abbeville. Their aircraft hit trees and the wreckage was found up to 1½ miles from the edge of the airfield. (Courtesy of Canadian virtual memorial)

The headstone of Flight Sergeant John Finlay McEwen, RCAF, Brookwood Cemetery, Surrey. (Courtesy of Canadian virtual memorial)

Bertie and Potter flew only twice in the month of November: over the night of 3–4 November, when no enemy activity was sighted and on the night of 10-11 November, when they slightly damaged a locomotive pulling freight south-east of Paris.

The 26 November saw a 100 per cent squadron take off, however Bertie did not fly on this occasion, although recognised the hard effort and achievement, writing a 'special order of the day' to his squadron.

> Congratulations to all ranks on the splendid effort put up by the Squadron last night. Bringing 17 aircraft to readiness and flying 54 hours, which is probably a record for an Intruder Squadron, reflects the greatest credit on all concerned. A stalwart effort such as this deserved more success, but we must take the Fortunes of war as they come, and if we keep our efforts at this high level, I feel confident we shall not lack for success in the future.

> B.R.O'B. Hoare
> Wing Commander, Commanding
> 605 Squadron, Bradwell Bay

Receiving a further signal from Air Marshal Sir Roderic Maxwell Hill, KCB, MC, AFC, giving praise for the squadron effort on the evening of 26 November.

> AO346, 27 NOV. The number of aircraft despatched on 'Flower' Operations last night by No 605 Squadron does great credit both to the aircrews and ground crews of your Squadron.

The Commanding Officer sent the following reply.

> A.3.28 Nov. Your AO.346 27 Nov. All aircrew and ground crews greatly heartened by your message and inspired to even greater efforts in the future.

On 3 December Bertie and Potter were flying towards the enemy coast on a sortie, Potter came up on the R/T reporting that he was feeling unwell and

Air Marshal Sir Roderic Maxwell Hill, KCB, MC, AFC, was Air Officer Commanding Commander-in-Chief of Fighter Command (also briefly called the Air Defence of Great Britain during his command) from 1943 to 1945. (Courtesy of RAF Commands)

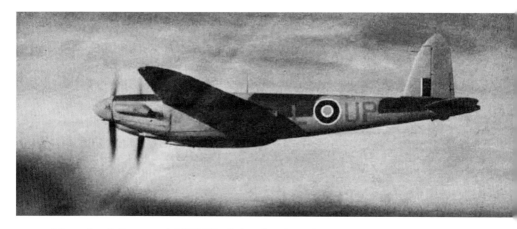

Mosquito *L-Love*, serial HJ779, flying in close formation, was flown by Bertie throughout 1943–44 while serving with 605 Squadron. (Courtesy of R. Rickard)

could not concentrate on carrying out his flying duties. Knowing this was not like Potter, Bertie turned for home twenty miles off the coast. This was to be the last operational sortie that Potter flew with Bertie, who was extremely reluctant to lose him as his Observer. Potter was posted to HQ, 9 Group, RAF Barton Hall, Lancashire, carrying out staff duties. It is unknown if the 'illness' was the reason for resting Potter from operations. However, he had distinguished himself on numerous tours, both on bombers and Mosquitos since the outbreak of the war.

On 10 December, flying with a new Observer, Flight Sergeant Kevin Mulcair, RCAF, Bertie crossed the Dutch coast low-level at 800ft, reaching the Dutch town of Westhoofd at 20:07, approaching their target, the Luftwaffe airfield at Gilze-Rijen. This airfield had been reported as one of the largest Luftwaffe bases in occupied North-West Europe. With no activity observed they flew to a further Luftwaffe airfield at Eindhoven, where they were met with a similar outcome. Returning to Gilze-Rijen at 20:37, they suddenly spotted a lone enemy aircraft. This was reported as a Do 217 preparing to land, with the aircraft last seen orbiting 500yds from Bertie's aircraft port nose.

> I throttled back, and turned to port, but the enemy aircraft did a steep turn to port also, and climbed away, passing us 250 yds range into the cloud base. The enemy aircraft went across the airfield and I saw him flash his D.R.L, but no more visuals could be obtained.

COMMANDING OFFICER 605 SQUADRON

Flight Sergeant Kevin
Joseph Mulcair,
RCAF. (Courtesy of
RAF Commands)

On 14 December several BBC war correspondents arrived at the squadron and wanted to prepare a broadcast on RAF Intruder operations. Recordings were made using gramophone recordings with mock Mosquito engines and gunfire in the background. This broadcast was played on the BBC European World service on 3 February 1944. Taking part, Bertie commented on his experience of Intruder operations and recalls the thrill and excitement of flying these types of dangerous missions over hostile territory.

> First of all, I should like to tell you not to measure the value of this night-fighter work over German aerodromes by the number of enemy aircraft known to have been destroyed. This is considerable, but I know positively that our mere presence over the enemy's bases has caused the loss of German bombers without even a shot being fired at them. Moreover, our presence upsets the Luftwaffe bomber organisation, throws their plans out of gear in many ways, and has a very big effect on the morale of the bomber crews. Night-fighter pilots chosen for this work are generally of a different type to the

ordinary fighter pilot. They must like night-fighting to begin with, which is not everybody's meat. They must also have the technique for blind flying, and when it comes to fighting, must use their own initiative and judgment, since they are cut off from all communications with their base and are left as free lances entirely to their own resources. Personally, I love it. Once up, setting a course in the dark for an enemy-occupied country, one gets a tremendous feeling of detachment from the world. And when the enemy's air base is reached there is no thrill, even in big-game shooting quite the same. You just hang about over their aerodromes and wait for them to come in and they are so frightened to find you there that they just pile themselves up, too easy. On goes the flare-path, a bomber comes low making a circuit of the landing field, lights on and throttle shut. A mile or two away, in our stalking Havoc, we feel our hearts dance. The throttle is banged open, the stick thrust forward, and the Havoc is tearing down in an irresistible

Bertie photographed in late 1943, the cheeky face says it all. (Author's Collection)

rush. One short burst from the guns is usually sufficient. The bomber's glide turns to a dive, the last dive it is likely to make. Whether you get the Hun or miss him, he frequently piles up on the ground through making his landing in fright.

Christmas day was enjoyed by all the squadron, and after Christmas lunch Officers, and ORs swapped clothes, reported in the squadron log: 'Resulting in complete chaos, no one quite knowing who the "real" officers were and who they were supposed to be saluting.' On 28 December saw Bertie recommended for an unusual award by his close friend and station commander of RAF Bradwell Bay, Wing Commander Russell Aitken, the award was the Order of Patriotic War 1st class, a Russian award first recognised on 20 May 1942 for distinction in combat. For fighter pilots it was a requirement to destroy a total of more than three aircraft in combat to be considered for this award, however, the Air Ministry would not allow the recommendation to go forward.

1944

On 2 January 1944, Bertie was recorded as the first RAF Intruder pilot to see the domestic lights of Sweden from the sky flying over Copenhagen, piloting Mosquito *L-Love*. Flying with Flying Officer Bob Muir as his Observer, they would go on to strike up quite a friendship over the remaining years of the war.

Muir recalls:

> I have just finished a tour completing thirty-five operations and looking forward to a rest. Wing Commander Hoare asked me to crew with him if he could get special dispensation from the Air Ministry, which he did, I did not have the guts to say 'NO!' Intelligence informed us that there was enemy flying near Kastrup, (Copenhagen, Denmark) but there was strong frontal 10/10 low cloud conditions and a pretty fierce north eastly wind. Sammy decided to 'have a go', so off we went. Flying blind, I fixed on GEE continuously until out of its range – refining our course accordingly, and was able to calculate the wind speed

and direction to apply to the remaining sea miles on D.R. After 2 hours 30 minutes 'blind' flying we cleared the front and there was Kastrup about 2 miles to port! A relieved Pilot said, 'Well done Bob', but there were no flying activities we returned to base.

Over the night of 10–11 January, Bertie and Muir made 605 squadron history by claiming the 100th enemy aircraft destroyed, while flying Mosquito *R-Roger,* over Chievres, Belgium. Patrolling over the target area they spotted a large aircraft off their nose, port side, heading south-east. Throttling back and sneaking in behind their unexpected prey, they identified it as a Ju188. The aircraft turned towards its airfields Visual Lorenz and Bertie commenced his attack:

> I attacked from the below and quarter astern, the enemy pilot, clearly obvious to his plight lowered his undercarriage. I gave him a 2–3 second burst with ½ ring deflections from about 800ft and strikes were seen on the fuselage.
>
> E/A went straight down and Intruder passed over the top, and sparks and flashes were seen as the E/A hit the ground 3½ miles east of the A/F at the village of CAMBRON ST VINCENT.
>
> Rounds fired:
> 32 HEI
> 37 S.API

Passing over the stricken bomber, Muir immediately called out on the R/T that they were under attack; however, this turned out to be the sparks and flames from the downed engaged aircraft as it hit the ground and exploded. Bertie was credited with a 'destroyed' for this engagement. Luftwaffe records show this aircraft crashing four miles east of Chievres, home to Staffel 1./KG 6, but this specific unit does not record any losses over these dates.

Muir recalls from this sortie: 'I plotted several legs so that we would arrive from the south and hopefully would be mistaken for one of their own German aircraft.'

Plans could now be laid for the inevitable party and presentation to which a number of past Commanding Officers would be invited, and

A Ju-188, similar type that Bertie claimed destroyed on the 10–11 January 1944. This aircraft was a high-performance medium bomber, with a better payload than the Ju 88. It was produced only in limited numbers for the Luftwaffe. (Courtesy of 12 OCH)

cordially entertained by the current serving members of the squadron. Many signals of praise and congratulations were sent to the squadron for their 100th victory and also recorded in squadron orders on the 13 January:

> A0320 11 Jan. Heartiest congratulations on the Squadron's Hundredth Hun and on your own achievement.
> Air Marshal Sir Roderic Maxwell Hill, KCB, MC, AFC

> Thanks for telegram. Heartiest congratulations to you on the Squadron's 100th Hun and W/Cdr. Hoare on his 8th victory which made the Century. County of Warwick Territorial Association and all Warwickshire will be very proud of your achievement and will I know wish to associate themselves most cordially with this message.
> Lord Willoughby de Broke, MC, AFC, Air Ministry

Heartiest congratulations to County of Warwick Squadron, to W/Cdr. Hoare in particular, on achievement of 100th Victory against the Hun. Birmingham and County very proud of its Squadron.

Lord Mayor of Birmingham

Well done 605 and its Commanding Officer
Sir W. Lindsay Everard MP, House of Commons, SW1

There was sad news when Bertie's previous Observer, Mulcair, now commissioned to the rank of Pilot Officer, was killed on operations on the 10 January, flying Mosquito *F-Fox*, serial HJ784, piloted by Flight Sergeant Richard Aldworth. They went missing on Intruder operations over Schiphol, Netherlands. Mulcair had flown with Bertie on several previous sorties.

Flying Officer Robert 'Bob' Muir. (Courtesy of RAF Commands)

A letter written by Bertie to the parents of Pilot Officer Kevin Mulcair of Montreal, Canada, of his loss while on operations. (Courtesy of Canadian virtual memorial)

Continuing to be acknowledged for his exemplary leadership and as Commanding Officer by his superiors, Bertie was awarded a Mentioned in Dispatches, gazetted in the *London Gazette* on 14 January 1944.

On 14 January both Bertie and Muir took off as part of a strong ten squadron aircraft contingent, participating in Operation Flower, flying in *L-Love* heading low over the Dutch coast. After investigating a series of Luftwaffe airfields at Wunstorf, Dunner-Zee, Vechta, Hesepe, and Nordhorn, many lights, including single flarepaths, flashing beacons admitting letters, 'UB' were observed. On their way home three searchlights and four AA flak guns engaged their aircraft, returning fire without any results.

SGT. OBS. KEVIN J. MULCAIR, R.C.A.F., has been reported missing after air operations overseas, according to word received here yesterday by his parents, John Mulcair, N.P., and Mrs. Mulcair, 3815 Marlowe avenue. Sgt. Obs. Mulcair had received part of his education at St. Leo's Academy, and was a student at Loyola College when he enlisted in the R.C.A.F. in June, 1941. He trained at Toronto, Oshawa, Hagersville, St. Johns, Mountain View, and Rivers, Man., where he received his wing in August, 1942. He went overseas shortly after. He is 23 years of age.

A Canadian Newspaper announcing the death of Pilot Officer Kevin Mulcair, interesting to note they still have him recorded as a SNCO. (Courtesy of Canadian virtual memorial)

Over the night of 21–22 January, with poor weather conditions, flying over an enemy airfield near the town of Stendal, central Germany. Bertie and Muir were peering into the target looking for lights of any enemy aircraft preparing to land or take-off. The following is taken from the combat report for this engagement.

> The target area was reached at 23:30 hours and a beacon was seen flashing 'F U' on the last bar of the E-W V/L (260'M). The V/L consisted of 13 lights with an arrowhead on the sixth and the eleventh. At 23:45 hours 6 whites were fired from an a/c 2 miles to the south of the A/F and 6 minutes later the headlight was seen coming down the V/L, this was doused as soon as it landed, which prevented the attack being pressed home. 5½ minutes later the a/c was seen taxying across the A/F in a southerly direction with its headlights on again. At 23:57 hours the Intruder attacked with a long burst from the starboard quarter at 2,000ft, strikes were seen and the lights were doused. Credited with 1 unidentified enemy aircraft damaged.

> Rounds fired:
> 63 Rds HEI
> 66 Rds S.API
> 86 Rds A.P
> 80 Rds Incd

Bertie flew a total of seven sorties throughout the month of February. One of these was on 3 February, flying with Muir overhead Brussels in Mosquito *L-Love*. One aircraft was 'damaged' and a second was reported as 'destroyed on the ground' at Le Culot. The following extract is taken from the combat report for this engagement:

> Two e/a were seen trying to land together but a double red from the ground caused both to put their navigation lights one and go round again. An attack at 06:32 hours was made one e/a from the front quarter with 2½ rings deflection but no strikes were observed. The second e/a landed and at 06:35 hours, a beam attack was made as it touched down, strikes

were seen on the fuselage and tail. This e/a is claimed as damaged. The A/F lights doused immediately after the attack and S/L's tried to engage. Another orbit of the A/F was made but nothing further was seen so a course was set for Le Culot which was reached at 06:44 hours. The V/L and F.P (290'M) and all A/F lights were on with a beacon flashing 'A0' 2 miles E of the A/F. Several a/c with D.R.L.s on were seen coming down the V/L during the next few minutes. At 06:50 hours

605 Squadron night flying schedule for night Intruder Ops dated 21 January 1944, note Bertie's and Muir's radio callsign 'Moisture 36'. (Courtesy of RAF Historical Branch)

two e/a were seen trying to land together, a red was fired from the ground and one landed with its navigation lights on. An attack was made from astern as it reached the end of the F.P, a long burst of cannon was given closing to about 600 feet, many strikes were seen all over the fuselage and starboard engine, large pieces flew off and the starboard nav light immediately went out. Owing to the number and concentration of strikes on the fuselage and starboard engine this e/a is claimed as probably destroyed. F/O MUIR is of opinion that the starboard wing fell off but W/C HOARE cannot corroborate this.

Rounds fired:
130 Rds HEI
136 Rds S.API

He was credited for one unidentified aircraft and one unidentified aircraft 'destroyed'. Over the night of 20–21 February, flying his beloved *L-Love,* with Muir next to him, Bertie was recorded on his 100th Intruder sortie, a statement that not many could claim. Flying overhead the Luftwaffe airfield at Soesterberg, Netherlands, he sighted a total of three enemy aircraft, one of these aircraft making a forced landing with its undercarriage raised on its final approach. Firing his cannon at a second aircraft, the following is taken from the combat report for this engagement.

This attack was head-on as it was taxying along the perimeter with its lights and headlight on. A long burst was given diving from 1,500 to 200ft. Many strikes were seen and all the A/C lights went out simultaneously. Judging by the wingspan it was a twin-engined A/C. As the Mosquito circled round a small fire was seen from the position of the combat, this was extinguished after about 10 minutes.

Bertie was credited with 'damaged' for this engagement. A third aircraft was briefly seen but lost in the darkness of the night. Official Luftwaffe records do not record any damaged aircraft landing at Soesterberg airfield over this date.

Two days later, on the night of 23 February, again flying with Muir, Bertie was carrying out Intruder operations over Leeuwarden, Netherlands, and hoping to intercept enemy aircraft at last light with Intelligence having reported aircraft returning from over the North Sea, escorting a German Kriegsmarine convoy close to the Dutch coast at Den Helder. Nothing was spotted over the Luftwaffe airfield and they flew a further forty miles west to the village of Egmond. Seeing nothing here either, they headed back to Leeuwarden for a second look. A shipping convoy was seen close to the Dutch coast, the ships fired their guns in an attempt to ward off the lone Intruder and were reported as being both 'heavy and light flak'. Over the night of 24–25 February, again flying with Muir over Luftwaffe airfields at both Beauvais and Evreux, little activity was sighted.

On 10 March, at RAF Bradwell Bay Station Commander, Wing Commander Russell Aitken and Bertie were invited to attend 'A' Flight celebrations. They held their long awaited 'flight party', which according to a member of the ground crew, Flight Sergeant Peter Freeman-Pannett, 'went off with quite a splash, W/Cdr Atkin and W/Cdr Hoare paid it a visit for a while and all got very merry. Drank all the beer and enjoyed it. 'B' Flight lost 'O' to-night.'

Bertie flew again over the night of 15–16 March, returning from a sortie over Germany, East of Stuggart, with poor weather conditions close to the city of Trier, flying with Muir. A transport locomotive was spotted pulling a long line of freight turning, towards their intended target they fired at a fast-moving string of carriages. Credited with a 'damaged' for this engagement.

605 Squadron broke an RAF record for a squadron in Fighter Command on the night of 15 March, inspiring a rather proud CO to congratulate the squadron by issuing a 'Special Order of the Day'.

> Congratulations to all ranks on the most outstanding achievement of last night. In reply to Bomber Command's request for maximum support, 22 aircraft and crews were brought to readiness, all of which went out on Intruder sorties, amassing the formidable total of over 102 night operational hours. Both the number of aircraft dispatched and the number of flying hours, is, by a very great margin, a record for any Squadron of Fighter Command of ADGB. During the course of these patrols 1 enemy aircraft was destroyed as well as a large number of trains and barges. To achieve these magnificent

results meant a tremendous amount of hard work on the part of every member of the Squadron as well as a very great number of personnel of 3094 Echelon and of the Station. Their willing co-operation and dogged hard work, coupled with their zeal and enthusiasm is deserving of the highest praise, for indeed without it the results could not have been obtained. The aircrew also responded in most splendid style and a special word of praise is due to the new members of the Squadron who acquitted themselves like veterans. I can only say again how greatly honoured and proud I am to command this redoubtable Squadron whose enthusiasm, morale and fighting spirit is second to none, and who, by their individual and collective efforts, spell disaster, damnation and destruction to the Hun.

Wing Commander B.R. O'B. Hoare, DSO DFC,
Officer Commanding 605 Squadron.

An extract taken from an undated letter written home:

We may not be allowed leave over Easter, so should be before that, or even after if you like that we meetup. I think the balloon won't go up before then, but you never know. We put up a tremendous effort the other night, we were asked for a maximum effort, in spite of me only meant to have 18 aircraft, I put up 22. I once did this before when I had 23 squadron. Only then we only put up 21 again out of 18! And this time the first 1,000 heavy four-engine bomber raid, some record doing it twice, and this time we achieved 102 hours, 40 minutes, operational night flying, nearly double the set record of any squadron in Fighter Command, and we put up the record, only a few weeks ago, this second 102 hours will I think never be beaten, as we are now we can put up 130 per cent of the aircraft. The distance we flew that night too was rather good, just more than once around the world. We have been, and are very busy, but going from strength to strength. I have got the decker back, and it is very good now, but it even suffers as yours does, the habit of occasional stopping and refusing to go for no reason.

Bertie and Muir shot down a Me 109 over Burg, late on the night of the 24–25 March when returning from operations over Stendal, Germany, carrying out an Operation Flower sortie. The following is taken from the combat report for this engagement.

> Mosquito VI UP-L took off from Bradwell Bay at 20:40 to patrol over STEND and BURG A/F's supporting Bomber Command's raid on BERIN. The Dutch coast was crossed at ALKMAAR at 21:35. STENADL was reached at 23:05. After flying round this A/F it was thought that presence of the Intruder was known and that consequently they were endeavouring to land at BURG so course was set for this A/F at 23:26. BURG was reached at 23:32, two e/a were seen to land but were not attacked, a third e/a was seen to land at 23:39 with its D.R.L. on and taxied in a N.W. direction across the A/F still with its D.R.L. on, this was attacked from the stern quarter. Fire was opened from 1,800ft, range 800yds. closing to 400ft height, 100yds range with one long burst of cannon and M.G. Many strikes were seen over e/a an explosion in centre of the fuselage occurred which threw debris in all directions. In the flash of the explosion F/O Muir recognised the e/a as a Me 109. Because of the shortage of fuel course was set straight back to STENDEL other e/a were seen with nav lights on in this area. Course was set for home at 23:47 and while passing SALZWEDEL at 23:52 the port motor failed and airscrew was feathered. The remaining 420 miles were flown on one motor, crossing out 5 miles S of EGMOND at 01:27 and landing at Woodbridge at 02:25 .

This action displayed the great flying ability of both aircrew, flying nearly 400 miles on only one engine and over hostile territory. It is unknown exactly what Staffel the Luftwaffe aircraft destroyed as a result of this engagement belonged to, research shows a single Me 109 from I./JG 300 received category 4 damage, destroyed by gunfire from an unknown RAF aircraft on an operational flight in the vicinity of where Bertie and Muir were reported to be operating. Muir recounts the engine failure they received during the night of 24–25 March:

The Port engine failed at Salzwedel – so 450 miles to Woodbridge on one motor. To keep the aircraft trimmed I had to position myself half-way out of my seat in a back-straining position with both feet on the rudder-bar. I remained in this position for three hours! Using my comprehensive flight plan I dog-legged the 'sitting suck' of an aircraft back to Woodbridge.

Bertie was awarded a second Bar to his DSO, gazetted in the *London Gazette* on 4 April 1944, becoming the only man in 605 squadron history to have received such an accolade.

This officer has participated in more than 100 sorties, involving attacks in airfields in Germany, Belgium, Denmark, Netherlands and France, escorts to bomber formations and a variety of other missions. He is a magnificent leader whose

A similar aircraft to the type destroyed by Bertie and Muir on the night of 24–25 March 1944. A captured German Messerschmitt Me 109G-6/U2 (Werk Nummer 412951) 'White 16' of 3./JG 301, one of two aircraft which landed in error at RAF Manston on 21 July 1944. Both fighters were on a night 'Wilde Sau' operation against RAF bombers. The pilot of this aircraft was Leutnant Horst Prenzel, Staffelkäpitan of 3./JG 301. (Courtesy of RAF Command Forum)

personal example of courage and devotion to duty has inspired all. In addition to his activities in the air, Wing Commander Hoare has devoted much of his energy and skill towards the training of other members of the squadron with excellent results. This officer, who has destroyed at least eight enemy aircraft, has rendered most valuable service.

Writing in a letter home, Bertie talks about the Bar to his DSO and his combat over the night of 24 and 25 March:

RAF Bradwell Bay
Essex
26 March 1944

Dearest Ma,

I thought I would ring you and tell you I got a bar to the DSO. By the time the call came through we were in the local having a party, bad show! On the same night as I got it I had to come home on one engine. This time nearly from Berlin but made it okay, thanks to my Observer, Bob, he was magnificent. We nearly had to bail out over there. But it all went well by the grace of God!

Now they are insisting I come off Ops, so I suppose you will be pleased, but I am heart broken.

All my love Rex

He continues ….

How did you like the raid last night? 90 Huns over, looking up. Young Hoare, who shot 2 down is in the other squadron here, and a good chap. As I was on my way out I heard him over the R/T. Just that he was closing in and was exultant! There goes another me, I had a crack at one but only a fleeting glance at him, as he taxied in and only damaged him. We had a very good night though. The whole squadron was out in the poor weather. We found all our targets, some 500 miles away, and all came back, a jolly good show. I was very surprised to hear in the New Year's honours list I got a Mention in Dispatches for my work in the year I was off Ops, and forming in the Intruder OTU. It's nice to think it was appreciated anyway.

I think I told you Sir Lindsay Everard, who is our Honorary Air Commodore, is presenting us with a silver model Mosquito to commemorate the 100th Hun, very jolly nice of him. It's been made by the Goldsmiths and Silversmiths and its even the letters and numbers of my aeroplane. I am going up to stay with him next week and so is Wing Commander Wright who was CO of 605. I used to know Wright before, he was an old pap staff at Reading, but don't suppose he will remember me.

The squadron departed RAF Bradwell Bay to their new home at RAF Manston on 7 April, with aircrew accommodated at Hurlingham Lodge on the seafront at Westgate. Taking their meals at nearby Doon Hall, reported in the squadron log: 'All concerned well were very pleased to leave the "splendid isolation" of Bradwell Bay, having hibernated there during the whole of winter.'

Bertie passed over command of the squadron to Wing Commander Norman John Starr on 10 April, reported in the official squadron history:

We regret the departure of W/C Hoare, who during his stay with us set a fine example to the offensive spirit prevailing in the Squadron. During his stay with us the Squadron's Bag was 33 destroyed, 2 Probably destroyed, 35 damaged. Men and women of the Squadron are sorry to see him leave would be a gross understatement considering how magnificently he had led the unit, and his place in 605 folklore would be assured. Starr, a very experienced Intruder pilot reported as coming with an excellent reputation and we feel sure he will maintain and improve the efficiency of the Squadron.

Bertie's last official duty with 605 was to attend a party at the Dorchester Hotel and be presented with a magnificent silver Mosquito model, a replica of the aircraft he was flying with Bob Muir on the date they engaged and shot down the squadron's 100th 'kill' in January. The party was held on

"Never Sleep" Squadron Dines on 100th Victim

ONE of the most successful home-based R.A.F. Intruder Squadrons—the No. 605 (County of Warwick) Auxiliary Air Force Squadron—which has for its motto "I Never Sleep," celebrated the destruction of its 100th victim with a dinner party at the Dorchester Hotel, London.

Twenty-six pre-war members of the squadron were the hosts and the guests were 30 members of the present squadron. Presiding over this group of past and present fighters was the honorary Air Commodore, Sir Lindsay Everard, M.P., who presented the members with a silver "Mosquito" bearing the identical marks of the machine flown by Wing Commodore B. R. O. B. Hoare when he completed the squadron's century of victims.

29 Pilots At First

Mobilised in 1939 with 29 pilots, the squadron helped to defend Scotland and North Sea shipping, battled at Dunkirk, and won about half its victories in the Battle of Britain.

Ordered abroad in 1941, it was chosen to defend the Dutch East Indies, where the members became prisoners of the Japanese.

Re-formed in 1942 and equipped with Boston Fighter-bombers the squadron became night intruders. Mosquitoes replaced Bostons and the "Never Sleeps" prowled over enemy territory, steadily building up their fine record.

A newspaper article documenting the party that 605 Squadron held at the Dorchester Hotel, London in celebration of the 100th claim. (Courtesy of R. Russell)

15 April and was attended by Air Commodore Sir Lindsay Everard MP, 605's Honorary Air Commodore, who kindly presented the trophy. Also present were seven former COs of the squadron including Air Commodore John Cecil Wright, Lord Willoughby de Broke, and two old friends, both pre-war officers, Air Commodore Lord Bearsted, and Air Commodore S.D. MacDonald.

The keeper of the squadron log kept up with his wit and good humour commenting on the Dorchester party:

> After the party broke up varied bands proceeded to the well-known and lesser known night haunts of London, returning to their beds at outlandish hours in the morning in many cases with little or no clues on the navigation entailed to proceed from point 'A' to point 'B'. No serious accidents or injuries were sustained.

The Dorchester Hotel party, Bertie is seated at the head of the table. (Courtesy of RAF Historical Branch)

The entrance to the Dorchester Hotel photographed in 1942. (Courtesy of Dorchester Hotel Archives)

Writing to his mother, Bertie recalls the impending move from 605 Squadron to take up a new posting.

> RAF Manston
> Kent
> 11.4.44
>
> Dearest Ma,
> Moved again, but I am still with the Squadron but shall be leaving in a few days for a station in Sussex I think. But I shall take some leave in before I go there I think, and I think I might go to Devon then.
> So, would you be ready by about Monday or Tuesday and I could, if it suits take you somewhere for a week or so? You are still allowed to go are you? I mean are there new regulations? Hasn't it been lovely weather? Real spring and warm too.
> I'll let you know exactly what is happening but don't know myself yet.
>
> Bye bye all my love
> Rex

Wing Commander Norman John Starr, DFC assumed command of 605 Squadron on the 10 April 1944. Starr was killed on the 8 January 1945. Due to marry Margot Goodwin, a VAD nurse, the following day, he took off in Anson MG552 with three wedding guests. At that time, the French port of Dunkirk was surrounded by Allied troops but remained in German hands until the end of the war, with fully functioning flak batteries. Within range, the Anson was shot down, Starr and the three passengers were all killed (Courtesy of Harold Starr)

Celebrating the 100th Intruder Victory of 605 Squadron at the Dorchester Hotel in London on 15 April 1944, centre is Group Captain Ceil Wright AFC, MP, founder of the 605 Auxiliary Squadron. On the right is Air Commodore Sir Lindsay Everard, MP, Honorary Air Commodore of the Squadron. (Courtesy of T. Cushing)

A photo taken at the Dorchester Hotel, enjoying a joke with Air Vice Marshal Edward Barker Addison, CB, CBE, FIEE, Air Officer Commanding 100 Group. (Courtesy of T. Cushing)

Air Commodore Sir Everard Lindsay, MP, presenting the silver Mosquito to Bertie. (Courtesy of T. Cushing)

The silver Mosquito presentation still remains with 605 RAuxAF Squadron, now based at RAF Cosford, Shropshire. (Courtesy of Shropshire Star)

STATION COMMANDER RAF LITTLE SNORING

Bertie's new posting was as Station Commander of an operational airfield with the unusual name of RAF Little Snoring, located in the county of Norfolk. Promoted to the temporary rank of Group Captain on 4 June, he arrived at Little Snoring on 8 June and took over command from Group Captain Leonard Cain Slee, who was posted close by, to RAF West Raynham, Norfolk.

Station Commander of
RAF Little Snoring.
(Courtesy of R. Russell)

With its unusual name of Little Snoring, the village derived from the first wave of Saxon invaders in around AD 450 and is recorded in the Domesday Book of 1085. Little Snoring is recorded by the names 'Esnaringa', 'Snaringa' and 'Snarlinga', named after 'Snare', the settlers' leader, and thus the name Little Snoring evolved over the centuries. It was the king's land with the main landholders being William de Warenne and Peter de Valognes, and the main tenant is said to be Ralph. Historically, the name Snoring Parva was used, 'parva' being Latin for 'smaller', nearby is located Great Snoring.

RAF Little Snoring was constructed in July 1943 as a satellite station and dispersal to nearby RAF Foulsham. In August, with the arrival of No.3 Group, full operational status was granted to the airfield. Lancasters of 115 Squadron arrived on 6 August shortly followed by 1678 Heavy Conversion unit from RAF East Wretham, Norfolk. November saw the airfield change command to be brought into 100 Group, and in January 1944 it was administrated by 100 Group HQ, located at Bylaugh Hall, Norfolk, which was centrally housed to administer its eight airfields across the county of Norfolk.

A photo of RAF Little Snoring taken from the cockpit of a Mosquito. (Courtesy of T. Cushing)

A group photo of HQ staff of 100 Group taken outside Bylaugh Hall, Norfolk. (Courtesy of 100 Group Association)

The 8 December 1943 saw 169 Squadron arrive from RAF Ayr, Ayrshire, flying Mosquitos, soon followed by 515 Squadron arriving on the 16 December from RAF Hunsdon, Hertfordshire. Initially flying Beaufighters, they converted to Mosquitos on their arrival at RAF Little Snoring. Both squadrons conducted night Intruder operations. 169 Squadron's stay was short lived and they departed RAF Little Snoring on 4 June 1944 for their new home of RAF Great Massingham, just a short distance away. They were soon replaced by 23 Squadron who had arrived by 2 June, having previously completing operations in the Mediterranean theatre.

Close proximity to the airfield was the tiny church of St Andrews, isolated and situated on the south-west side of the airfield. Already abandoned when Bertie first arrived at RAF Little Snoring. Having strong religious beliefs, he decided that the church would be restored to its former glory by 'self-help' ground parties from the station, who assisted with the restoration. It was reinstated to become the station church, with the first official church parade being held on 16 July, with the service conducted by Squadron

23 Squadron posing in front a Mosquito at RAF Little Snoring, the control tower can be seen to the rear right of the photo. (Courtesy of T. Cushing)

RAF Little Snoring, the photo being taken from the control tower showing dispersed Mosquito aircraft. (Courtesy of T. Cushing)

St. Andrews Church, Little Snoring. (Courtesy of Round Towers)

Leader, Reverend Leonard William Goulding, the station chaplain. Regular services were held every Sunday thereafter, by all who were available, some reluctantly attending, marching from station HQ to the church.

One of Bertie's first duties was not flying, but to help a local farmer collect his crop, recorded in 23 Squadron log:

> Quite a number of aircrew, including the Commanding Officer, are helping a local farmer with the Pea Harvest. But it looks as though their rate of picking at a price of 2/9d per bag is not going to be very remunerative. Perhaps when they had had a little more experience they will improve. Anyway, the main object is a change and plenty of fresh air coupled with the 'Odd Noggin'.

Bertie's next recorded sortie was flying with 515 squadron over the night of 5–6 July, in his Mosquito *B-Bertie*, with Flight Lieutenant Bill Gregory as his Navigator. Flying in the overhead of Luftwaffe airfields at Laon, Couvron, and finally Cambrai, in Northern France. At the final location, the enemy airfield was seen to be active, with a lit runway and white flares

A captured Bf 110 photographed at RAF Little Snoring, reported in the Station log on 8 August, as. 'The "circus" visited the station.' This particular aircraft was captured in Denmark and when it made its maiden flight to Britain, its undercarriage failed and had to be lowered for the entire flight. It was flown to various RAF airfields around the country to teach RAF night fighter pilots its capabilities and weaknesses. The circus also included a captured Me 109 and Ju 88. (Courtesy of T. Cushing)

being fired into the sky. At 02:23, at an altitude of 2,000ft, a locomotive was spotted travelling slowly on the St Gobain branch line of the Noyon-Laon Railway, and it was attacked twice with the train coming to an immediate standstill. The engine was seen to be pouring out steam, continuing to circle the crippled train after the attack, with little results. Bertie was credited with a 'damaged' for this engagement.

Flying again on 10 July, with Squadron Leader Geoffrey Bond, the Station Navigation Officer as his Navigator, flying *B-Bertie* in a 2-ship formation with Mosquito No 161, the second aircraft was crewed by Squadron Leader Paul Rabone and Flight Lieutenant Frederick Johns.

The following is taken from 515 squadron log for this engagement:

> These aircraft successfully completed a day 'Ranger' patrol of Schleswig-Holsten area. When north of Peelworm at 18:59 aircraft No 161 attacked a small motor launch with one second burst of cannon. Strikes recorded, launch stopped, smoke appeared and launch 'settled' down. At 19:03 a tug appeared

off the Isle of Fohr, and a 3 second burst from aircraft No 161 scored hits on the superstructure. A minute later off Wyk, a machine gun post was shot up with 3 second burst of cannon, 2 huns and tent disappeared.

As Station Commander, Bertie would commence the start of each mission briefing and personally wish each crew good luck before they taxied out onto the runway. This ritual was fondly remembered by members of 23 squadron.

> In the Op's room, the station commander was there on the stage, he would give us the information with possibly a bit more from the intelligence officer. Behind the stage was a huge map of enemy territory so that our respective routes etc could be displayed. He would start with, 'Gentlemen, there will be flak, almost certainly quite heavy flak. If you cannot go over, you will go under. If you cannot go under – you will go through!'

More humour was seen at RAF Little Snoring when Bertie banned the use of shotguns, rifles, and pistols by all RAF personal, recalled by a member of 23 squadron:

> We were settling into Little Snoring, though we did have some problems living together in our crowded living conditions. With cold concrete floors and an unheated Nissen hut, one was reluctant to get out of bed. With the light bulb in the centre and its switch hanging off that light. If I remember rightly it was Baron Goldie who should have got out of bed to do this on one particular occasion. Instead, he produced his .38 revolver and started shooting at the electric light bulb. He kept missing, but others produced their guns and tried to do better. The next result was that in the end somebody had to get out of bed and switch off the light in the proper fashion. After that, the roof leaked furiously when we had a downpour. This happened on more than one occasion until Flight Lieutenant Griffith went one better. He came back from leave with a shotgun. By this time, the works department was rather fed up and the Commanding Officer banned shotguns and firing bullets at our hut's light bulbs.

Antics continued, even with senior officers joining in. A Flight office was about 200yds from 515 Squadron B Flight office. Squadron Leader Paul Rabone decided to playfully shoot a .303 bullet just above the head of Squadron Leader Henry Morley in the B Flight office. After this incident Morley was sure to keep his blinds firmly closed.

Bertie was promoted to the temporary rank of Wing Commander on 1 July 1944, gazetted in the *London Gazette* on 21 July 1944. As one of the first duties as Station Commander, Bertie had to place one of his most experienced pilots under 'close arrest' on 26 July. Squadron Leader Robert Moore, serving with 515 Squadron, was posted to Station HQ pending discipline charges. It cannot be verified, but it is believed that he had got drunk, and flown a Mosquito low over an official parade at RAF Elmdon, Warwickshire. Reported in the Station Log: 'Charges of breaches of flying discipline and conduct to the prejudice of good order and discipline'. He was released from 'close arrest' to 'open arrest' five days later and finally released from this action on 1 August on authority of AOC 100 Group,

105 L–R Bertie, Flight Lieutenant 'Joe' Huggins, Flying Officer Hamilton-Smith, Squadron Leader John Penny. (Courtesy of T. Cushing)

Left: Squadron Leader Robert Henry Moore, DFC, an experienced RAF pilot, completing a total of thirty-five operations with 11 Squadron, on 17 June 1941, leading a formation of three Blenheim Bombers against the Vichy French destroyer *Vaquelin*, harboured in Beirut, Greater Lebanon. Achieving six direct hits, killing five of the sailors, Moore's aircraft was badly shot up with his Observer badly injured. (Courtesy of T. Cushing)

Below: A photo taken from Moore's aircraft of bombs impacting the Vichy French targets on 17 June 1941, which earned him the DFC. (Courtesy of RAF Commands)

reported to be selected for Court Martial on 20 September. However, this outcome did not occur, and it is believed that Moore was suffering from early stages of PTSD. He was posted on 25 October to No.7 FIS at RAF Upavon, Wiltshire.

Bertie was flying over 5 and 9 August, and on the first of these dates, he flew *B-Bertie* with Gregory as his Navigator. However, due to his aircraft suffering from jammed elevators, they had to return early from the sortie, reported in 23 Squadron's log, 'all aircraft sailed forth; unluckily the Station Commander had to land at Colerne due to jammed elevators'.

Two days later, on 11 August, again piloting his beloved *B-Bertie* with his Navigator, Flying Officer John Smith, he was flying as part of a formation of six Mosquitos escorting Lancasters of No 5 Group tasked with bombing the port area of Bordeaux, south-west France. Reported as rendezvous with the bombers at 15:25 at an altitude of 18,000ft and a latitude and longitude of 4650N 0250E. The Mosquitos were to accompany the bomber formation over the target area and depart them on completion of the mission at Quiberon Bay, refuelling their aircraft at RAF Winkeligh, Devon, before returning to RAF Little Snoring, the sortie totalling 9½ hours.

Flying Officer John Smith DFC, nicknamed 'Lucky Jack', flew with Bertie on the 11 August on a sortie over the French port area of Bordeaux. He was KIA on the night of 21/22 November with his pilot, Flight Lieutenant Frederick L'Amie DFC, flying Mosquito PZ344, which was hit by flak and crashed nearby the small town of Walbeck, close to Geldern, near the Dutch-German border. Both crew were buried in a joint grave at Rheinburg Cemetery. (Courtesy of T. Cushing)

Opposite and above: 23 Squadron Mosquitos refuelling at RAF Winkleigh, Devon on 11 August. (Courtesy of T. Cushing)

Mosquito FB.VI, *B-Bertie*, serial PZ176, with an ASH radar fitted to the nose, recorded as a 23 Squadron aircraft parked on northern dispersal site at RAF Little Snoring, with ground crew standing in front of its nose. Standing on the left of the group, the unnamed airman did not want to be in the photo as he felt he was not smart enough, having just completed an oil change on this specific aircraft. On the crew door can be seen the Hoare family crest, the family motto reads, '*Venit hora*', translating to. 'The hour has come'. (Courtesy of R. Russell)

Bertie was very particular with who he flew with on operations; on one occasion a junior pilot from 23 squadron, Flying Officer Douglas Badly was tasked to fly with him on a transit flight back to RAF Little Snoring. Badly recalls his nervous flight back:

> I flew his aircraft once to pick him up at Liverpool. It had the odd little curtain over one or two of the instruments just to cut down the brightness of the luminous paint to help with the night vision. On the way back he flew and I navigated. There was almost, but not quite, total cloud cover and Sammy flew above it. I was using the odd pinpoint through the odd hole and mental arithmetic. I am sure that he was being awkward, after a very long silence he said, 'do you know where you are?' I told him that if he dived down thorough the cloud then and there he should find himself over Little Snoring. He complied and luckily, there underneath us was our airfield. Sammy did not say a word, not even a thank you for all my day's effort.

Another 23 Squadron pilot, Flying Officer George Stewart, was returning to RAF Little Snoring from a sortie with engine failure. Attempting to land his stricken Mosquito he veered off the end of the runway with his aircraft undercarriage collapsing. With all future emergencies, and for any aircraft with damage, Bertie deemed the runway too short to land and they would have to divert to a nearby airfield. Many of the other pilots disagreed and felt the runway was an acceptable length; on three occasions, Flying Officer Douglas Badly landed his badly crippled aircraft, the last of these he was flying Bertie's very own aircraft *B-Bertie*. He recalls:

> One night I had set out to do an operation in Sammy's own YP-B, but we were all recalled possibly because of the fog coming in. It did not matter too much, as the propellers' constant speed unit went mad and I had to return on one engine. I, of course, landed back at Little Snoring but Sammy did not complain as he had his aeroplane back. After the arrival of Jock Wilson, I had to land there a couple of times on one engine.

Bertie's good fortune continued over the night of 29–30 August, conducting an Intruder sortie flying with 23 Squadron, piloting *B-Bertie,* with Gregory as his Navigator. Taking off late evening in good weather as part of a formation of sixteen Mosquitos, they headed low over the Danish coast and towards their respective targets. Over the Luftwaffe airfield at Herning in mid-Jutland, Bertie damaged two unidentified aircraft taxiing on landing, one was reported to have two engines. After this attack the lone Intruder attacked a dummy airfield at Skinderholm near Sunds and attacked two dummy airplanes. The dummy airfield was equipped with dummy aircraft that could move on the ground, with lights attached. They were equipped with pyrotechnics that could be activated so that it looked as if the plane had exploded. It was serviced by three elderly soldiers of the Wehrmacht.

Operation Overlord saw the successful invasion of North-West Europe on 6 June 1944 off the Normandy coast, giving the Allied forces a secure foothold on the Continent. This meant RAF operations could forward mount from captured Luftwaffe bases, allowing a longer flying time over enemy territory. One such sortie was over 3–4 September; as usual, Bertie was piloting *B-Bertie*, with Gregory as his Navigator. The following is taken from Bertie's combat report for this sortie:

> Mosquito took off from CAEN/CARPIQUET at 21:30 hours and landed there on return at 04:00 hours. Arrived Liz area at 00:20 hours in ten-tenths and cloud at 500ft and raining (tail and front). Complete inactivity in the area, and no E/A were seen. On the way back, the MUNICH area was visited and in the light of good moon, METTENHEIM A/F (4816N 1229E) was clearly seen. In the NW dispersal, a number of E/A were parked, and at 00:45 hours the first of seven attacks was made on the aircraft with cannon and machine gun from 1,200-500ft. Strikes were recorded on at least THREE unidentified S/E E/A and TWO T/E E/A, and these are claimed as damaged. Mosquito then proceeded to MAISACH A/F (4813N – 1116E) which was well the bright moon. A S/E E/A was seen on the A/F, and at 01:12 hours this was attacked with machine guns from about 1,000 to 500ft. Strikes were registered, and this A/C is claimed as damaged.

No Flak or S/L was encountered.

CLAIM: Four unidentified S/E E/A

Two unidentified T/E E/A

ARMAMENT: 680 rounds of 20mm cannon (170 per cannon)

2,000 rounds of .303 (500 per Browning)

No Stoppages

Camera exposed

WEATHER: No cloud, and bright moonlight, except in LINZ area where ten-tenths cloud – base 500 feet – prevailed.

Fürstenfeldbrück is the name of the Luftwaffe airfield that was attacked, located close to the small village of Maisch.

Bertie had some very unique characteristics; he was best known across the RAF Intruder community for his large handlebar moustache, which was reported to be 6 inches from 'wingtip to wingtip'. Bertie commented, 'Huh! Fluff, my boy. If both ends couldn't be seen from behind, it isn't worth the name "handlebar".' Some believed it was the biggest moustache in the entirety of the RAF; when needing to put on his oxygen mask when flying, the tips stuck up outside on either side and it was described by pilots as looking like a large beetle on his face.

A 23 Squadron Mosquito flying in close formation on an operational sortie from RAF Little Snoring. (Courtesy of T. Cushing)

A station order brought into force by Bertie, and very unpopular with many pilots, concerned their escape photos in case they were shot down over occupied territory. He ordered that all moustaches and facial hair had to be removed, to look 'less British'. So, for example, if escaping through Spain, you could pass off as a local. Bertie, of course, was very proud of his moustache and some people came close to challenging his supremacy in that particular field. Wing Commander Alan 'Sticky' Murphy, Commanding Officer 23 Squadron, was perhaps his biggest challenger on the Station, and all were sure that this escape photo ploy was to quash Bertie's opposition. Murphy just clipped enough ends off to pass as a continental.

Another distinguishing trait was the result of the accident in October 1939 – the loss of his total eyesight in one eye. Many pilots took bets on which of the eyes was the real one and which one was the glass one; the problem was exacerbated by one eye being blue and the other brown. Many members from both squadrons could not understand how he managed to pilot an aircraft, and ultimately how he could see and attack targets at night! A 23 squadron pilot commented: 'I had tried attacking at night with one eye closed and couldn't manage judging the range. I concluded that it was decidedly dangerous, with the risk of collision. There was no doubt about it. He was definitely a fine fighter pilot!'

His final attribute was the steep angle at which he wore his service cap, always wearing his 'lucky cap', as remembered with humour by one of the groundcrew, LAC Tom Hodgson. On one occasion, Bertie was returning from an RAF airfield in the North of England in a Mosquito and Hodgson was marshalling the aircraft into its dispersal; when the aircraft engines ceased, Bertie got out of the cockpit and realised he had left his 'lucky hat' at the airfield. He told Hodgson to refuel his aircraft and that he would fly back and retrieve it – which he did.

Between September and December, both 23 and 515 squadrons were fitted with the VI/centimetric AI Mk XV combination (Air-to-Surface Homing), abbreviated to ASH radar. AI Mk XV started life as a maritime search radar and, as applied to 100 Group aircraft, it took the form of a 5-ft long 'bomb' that was mounted in the aircraft's nose in place of the Mosquito's four forward-firing machine guns. In the hands of a skilled operator, AI Mk XV could detect targets at a maximum range of 3.75 miles and track them down to a minimum range of 600ft. The set could also produce an 'H2S-like' ground picture that was most useful for navigation. Of the cited

Above left: A cartoon sketch of Bertie, this capturing his large handlebar moustache and his distinctive hat tilt. (Courtesy unknown artist)

Above right: A pencil sketch of Bertie when he was Station Commander at RAF Little Snoring, drawn by the well-known artist, Pat Rooney. (Courtesy of R. Russell)

Left: Bertie's distinctive eye variation, following his accident in October 1939. (Courtesy of RAF Historical Branch)

LAC Tom Hodgson on the left of the photo, standing with a fellow member of groundcrew in front of Mosquito *D-Dog* at RAF Little Snoring. (Courtesy of T. Cushing)

units, 23 Squadron aircraft were fitted with ASH, GEE, MONICA and the PERFECTOS IB homer and despatched on its first operational low-level AI Mk XV sortie during December 1944. 515 Squadron despatched its first AI Mk XV sortie during January 1945, at which time, it was intended to team its ASH radars with a MONICA tail warner. In the event, this proposal came to nothing. Due to Bertie's poor eyesight, he could never fly with this equipment fitted and it was a daily task to change the nose section and add or remove the ASH radar nose, depending on who was flying *B-Bertie*.

An ASH Radar being installed to the nose section of an unknown Mosquito aircraft at RAF Little Snoring. (Courtesy of R. Russell)

Bertie's close friend at RAF Little Snoring was Wing Commander Alan 'Sticky' Murphy, Commanding Officer, 23 Squadron. Alan was a very experienced RAF pilot, having joined 1419 Special Duties Flight in 1941, perfecting short take offs and landings, and dropping off SOE agents into occupied Europe. He was seriously wounded in the neck on one of these dangerous missions when his Lysander aircraft was ambushed by Germans waiting for him on the ground. He managed to take off and safely return to his home airfield. Converting to Mosquitos in 1943 and initially posted to Malta to 23 Squadron where he took part in numerous night attacks, believing the squadron motto, '*Semper Aggressus* – Always on the attack', which he was more inclined to translate as 'Right lads! After the bastards.' Taking command of the squadron, he returned to RAF Little Snoring and led from the front at all times.

Tragically, Murphy was killed on a sortie on 2 December 1944 flying over Zwolle, Netherlands, piloting Mosquito serial PZ456, with his Navigator Flight Sergeant Douglas Darbon. Taking off from RAF Little Snoring to conduct Intruder operations over Luftwaffe airfields around the Gutersloh region of Germany. Heavy flak guns had been situated in the vicinity of the industrial area of Zwolle. Regularly Mosquito aircraft would swoop in low and 'shoot up' the marshalling yard. The defending Germans named these low level attacks the 'daily milk run'. It is believed on this occasion Alan was shot down by these defending guns. Nothing was heard from the lone Intruder and when past their landing time, they were reported as missing. Air Sea Rescue sorties were carried throughout the next day but no survivors were located and all were forced to cease searching due to poor weather conditions over the North Sea and English Channel. Murphy was fondly remembered by all that knew him and became loved for his humanity, daring leadership, and natural charm to all.

Darbon was not Alan's regular Navigator, usually this was Flight Lieutenant Robert 'Jock' Reid. However, on the night of 2 December, Jock had been suffering from earache and could not fly, he recalls:

I met the Commanding Officer going into the mess for lunch. 'We're flying tonight' he said. I then told him I was grounded for a few days because I had seen the MO that morning. 'That's OK – we'll just scrub it,' Murphy said. It was 10 o'clock on Sunday morning before I knew Sticky had gone flying and who had gone with him. When I met some of the boys who were at church, they said, 'Oh, so you got back'. I replied that I hadn't been anywhere. I didn't even know the Flight Sergeant who was his Navigator that night.

It was reported earlier on that day that Murphy had visited his friends, the Andersons, at a farm nearby, but they were out. Caretaker Eric Myhill had watched as Murphy rocked up and down on his heels in front of the log fire roaring in the grate. He noticed that the Wing Commander was wearing his favourite American brown flying boots. 'Tell Mr and Mrs Anderson I'll be back tomorrow', he had told him. 'Jock' Reid always felt guilty for the death of his pilot and believed if he had been flying that night he would have stopped Murphy going over the area of Zwolle and would have survived the sortie.

The tragic news of Murphy's death hit Bertie immensely hard and he personally broke the news to Murphy's wife, Jean, who was living in nearby Fakenham at the time of her husband's death. However, 'There was no mourning, spirits were kept up.'

On 3 December, 23 Squadron held a squadron 'bash', reported in 23 squadron log:

> The Squadron was stood down for the night, the information coming through quite early in the morning. Consequently, it was decided to hold a party, and just before lunch many squadron members were to be seen making for the Bar. By mid-afternoon it was in full swing, and carried on until long after midnight, a good time being had by all.

Bertie was promoted to substantive rank of Wing Commander on 4 December 1944, gazetted in the *London Gazette* on 12 January 1945. Fog and low cloud did not halt Christmas day at RAF Little Snoring, described as a lively affair, with Bertie enjoying some leave before returning to the station to join in the festive celebrations, recorded in the 23 Squadron log on 25 December:

Wing Commander Allan 'Sticky' Murphy, DSO + Bar, DFC, was Officer Commanding 23 Squadron, and a close friend to Bertie when stationed at RAF Little Snoring. (Courtesy of T. Cushing)

L–R, Facing, Wing Commander Allan 'Sticky' Murphy and Bertie in the officers mess at RAF Little Snoring. (Courtesy of T. Cushing)

Xmas day! And a general stand down was ordered for everyone in the Group. The 'LANC' crews were still with us, having been unable to 'get off' as yet. The bar opened at 11:00 and by 11:10 hours one could neither get in or out of the bar except by climbing over the counter. Most of the sergeants came over for the usual Xmas session which developed in a real party.

At midday, the officers were asked to return the visit to the sergeants' mess which was immediately accepted …. And a real session was soon in operation there. Suddenly someone suggested that it was about time we served the airmen's dinner …. and a battalion of officers and NCOs made their way to the airmen's mess. Including the 'LANC' aircrews[*]. The meal was a feast never to be forgotten, together with the

---

[*] Reported in the station log. *'We were 'blessed' on Christmas Eve with a diversion in the form of thirteen Lancasters from 622 Squadron, RAF Mildenhall.*

antics of FARREL and PRICE who sang many songs and insisted they should finish each one by singing, 'Oh I had to ring you up this morning cause I couldn't sleep a wink last night.' This created a raucous turmoil and everyone joins in the two lines.

Our own dinner came around 18:00 hours and was a spread on its own. Quite a number of officers sat down and enjoyed the meal. Some idiot passed round a plate for a collection for the cooks, this disgusting act creating silence when finally, the plate reached the PMC, SQN LDR PRICE, who in a rage left his place at the table and proceeded to the culprit complete with plate and money. A tense silence reigned. Was he mad! The rest of the evening appeared to be a bit of a flop. ENSA party didn't turn up, and so many spent the night sat around the fire.

Many aircrews helped entertain 108 children who attended the special Christmas party on 24 December. With Santa Claus arriving by aeroplane to give the presents from the Christmas tree, the children's excitement was intense, and everyone had a wonderful time.

Above and opposite: A typical party scene at RAF Little Snoring, this specific theme being pirates with captions such as 'Skip's log' written on the ship's wheel, this was believed to be in relation to a section of wood that was located in the tail wheel of Bertie's aircraft on return from a sortie, displaying the low level altitude he was flying at. (Courtesy of T. Cushing)

Right: A menu for Christmas dinner held at RAF Little Snoring on 25 December 1944. (Courtesy of T. Cushing)

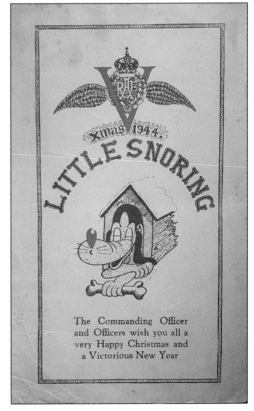

Xmas 1944.

LITTLE SNORING

The Commanding Officer and Officers wish you all a very Happy Christmas and a Victorious New Year

133

Over the night of 28–29 December, Bertie flew Mosquito serial PZ178, tail number unknown with Flight Sergeant John Redwood as his Navigator, carrying out a Night Ranger mission over the Northern Austrian city of Linz, with weather conditions recorded in 23 squadron log as 'hopeless'.

In early 1945, Bertie, writing home to his mother, described how he could see the end of the war approaching and his thoughts on this end of hostilities.

> Dear Ma,
>
> We are still very busy although targets for us are now getting fewer and fewer, and Huns as well. I must confess I shall not be sorry a bit when this is all over. I have had about enough, and I am tired, and I feel I would really like a long rest. To recuperate, I wonder if I will get it?
>
> I went for a dinner in London with some friends, I flew to Northolt, got a train to London, and then a train back to Northolt, and flew back again all in one evening. Everybody considered me mad for doing this!

Wing Commander Gerald Joseph Constable Maxwell, MC, DFC, AFC, DL, was a First World War fighter ace, he was Station Commander at RAF Ford between 1941 and 1945. (Courtesy of RAF Commands)

Last week I was down at Ford, Gerald Maxwell being invalided out of the RAF and Ford gave a dinner for him to which all the officers that served under him were invited, it was a most enjoyable evening. Gerald's speech was simply wonderful, and absolutely typical and unique. I enjoyed it especially as I was not forced to drink too much as one generally is, nowadays I simply can't take drink and feel quite ill. Folks' hospitality by forcing drink on me is in fact quite the reverse, no one can understand this.

The same day at Ford I gave a lecture to the night fighter leaders' school, which is now there, on Intruding. So could thus kill two birds with one stone. I have agreed to give a lecture to every course so I hope to get home for a night the next time I come down in about 5 weeks' time.

1945

Throughout the month of January and the early part of February, 23 squadron got familiarly with their new ASH radar fitted into their aircraft; for Bertie, station duties remained his priority, and he was awarded a further MID on 1 January. Bertie began to accept the war was nearing its end and he started to decrease his operational tempo. He carried out a Night Ranger on 23 February over Northern France and a further Night Ranger on 25 February, on both occasions flying Mosquito *V-Victor**, with Squadron Leader Bob Muir as his Navigator, forward mounting from RAF Gravesend, Kent, followed by the now liberated airfield at Juvincourt, Northern France, early during the daylight hours.

On the sortie of 23 February, piloting his lone Intruder low over the Austrian city of Salzburg, Bertie reached the target area of Loffingen, claiming a locomotive and its freight carriages 'damaged', and a further military vehicle convoy 'destroyed'. A further two convoys were also 'damaged'. This specific target was believed to be a large German ammunition storage depot. Fires and explosions were started from 80 x 4lb incendiaries bombs.

The sortie on 25 February saw both crew have a lucky escape over enemy territory when, again flying Mosquito *V-Victor** on a Night

Ranger over Lake Chiem, Germany, their first bit of trouble started. Muir recalls:

> One motor failed at Lake Chiem, restarting after 20 minutes, but only half capacity. 1 x 100 gallon tank refused to jettison and we were failing to make height. Luckily it fell off when the mountain peaks were very near! It was clear moonlit night so had to map read through the Alpine valleys to our French base! If I say it myself, it was no mean feat!

Life at RAF Little Snoring carried on as normal as well as Bertie's station responsibilities, recorded in 23 squadron log on 6 March.

> This week sees the start of 'PT. WHILE YOU WORK' in most cases for ground personnel, it's a period of fifteen minutes three times per week, and for the aircrew, two compulsory periods of one hour duration per week.

A momentous date for Bertie was over the night of 23–24 March when he flew his last operational sortie flying Mosquito *R-Roger**, with Muir as his Navigator. Taking off with eight other aircraft from RAF Little Snoring to carry out a Ranger sortie, they visited a number of Luftwaffe airfields over Northern Germany. They reached Wesendorf airfield at 23:50 where little activity was sighted. Flying low at 1,000ft, Bertie proceeded to release incendiaries on a small taxi track on the south-east side of the airfield, with explosions observed striking the intended target.

A prestigious date was recorded in the station log on 1 May, when the Station WAAF section was selected to compete in the 'The Sunderland Cup', awarded annually to the most efficient WAAF Section across RAF Bomber Command:

> We had been chosen, as the best WAAF Section 100 Group, to represent the Group in the final of the Sunderland Cup Competition. Excitement ran high and everyone made great efforts to put up a 'Good show' on 30th May. Whether we win

---

* *Muir's Logbook states these aircraft were coded* V-Victor *for the sorties flown both 23 and 25 February and* R-Roger *on 23 March, this is written different to both 23 and 515 Squadron 540 ORBs, stating these aircraft were both tail number 548.*

or lose, it was felt that the Section did credit to 100 Group and at the end of the visit we received congratulations from the judges.

Group Officer Beecroft (Air Ministry) and Group Officer Bather (Bomber Command) on 30 May 1945, to judge the Section for the Sunderland Cup Competition. Group Captain Porte, OBE and Squadron Officer Ford O.B.E, visited also.

June – The WAAF birthday this month brought a most interesting visit – that of the deputy director WAAF to present the Sunderland cup. With her were Group Captain Beecroft, inspector general of WAAF, Group Captain Bather of Bomber Command, Air-Vice Marshal E.B. Addison, AOC 100 Group and Air Commodore R.C. Spencer, D.A.O.A. of Bomber Command. The whole station was on parade for the event and the march-past was headed by the WAAF section.

After the presentation the WAAF personnel were entertained to a special tea for which there was a 4-tier birthday cake, made by one of the RAF cooks from ingredients supplied by all messes. In the evening a Gala dinner was held which everyone voted the day as the 'best ever'.

Left to right – Group Officer Elizabeth Bather, WAAF Staff Officer, Bomber Command; Flight Officer Constance Gallavan, Officer in Charge of WAAF Section at Little Snoring, Group Officer Constance Woodhead, Deputy Director, WAAF, inspecting a barrack hut. (Courtesy of T. Cushing)

Above and opposite top: The parade of the presentation of the 'Sunderland Cup' which was held at RAF Little Snoring on 30 May 1945. Standing on the podium from L–R Group Officer Constance Woodhead, Air Commodore Geoffrey Spencer, Air Vice-Marshal Edward Addison, and Bertie. (Courtesy of T. Cushing)

L–R Front Row: Flight Officer Helen Jessie Kitson of RAD Chipping Warden, Squadron Officer Margaret Wallace Wright Ford of 100 Group, Group Officer Elizabeth Constance Bather of HQ Bomber Command, Group Officer Constance Woodhead, Deputy Director WAAF, Flight Officer Constance Lilian Gallavan of Little Snoring, Group Officer Beryl Constance Beecroft, Inspector General WAAF. Back Row: Section Officer Nellie Sophy Henry Reynolds of Little Snoring, Section Officer Diana Paget Black of Little Snoring, Flight Officer Mary Hyde-Parker of HQ Bomber Command, Section Officer Jane Elvira MacLeod of Little Snoring, and Section Officer Hylda Marion Hamilton of Little Snoring. (Courtesy of T. Cushing)

Group Officer Constance Woodhead, Deputy Director WAAF, presenting the Sunderland Cup to Flight Officer Constance Gallavan, officer in charge of the WAAF Section at Little Snoring.

Bertie's dine out in the Junior Ranks' Dining Hall, RAF Little Snoring, Bertie seated at the head of the table. (Courtesy of T. Cushing)

Finally departing RAF Little Snoring as Station Commander at the beginning of August, Bertie had many fond memories of his time. He was relieved by Wing Commander Phil Russell. Recorded in the station log:

> Group Captain Hoare would always be fondly remembered as being extremely modest about himself. Taking great pride in his station. His keenness and determination were infectious and insured that his station was always sure to give a very good account of itself in all aspects of station life. He conveyed his enthusiasm and his pride in the service to all.

Mosquito losses based at RAF Little Snoring were extremely high, with 23 Squadron losing a total of twenty-one crews and 515 squadron, a total of ten, a psychological burden that never left Bertie. As Station Commander he did not have to fly any operational sorties, but it was in his nature as an Intruder pilot to do so, commenting: 'I could not send crews out to fight, and risk their lives, and not do it myself!'

Cover sheet from Bertie's dine out from RAF Little Snoring, August 1945.
(Courtesy of Muir family)

BERTIE'S AND LUCY'S WEDDING

A Norfolk couple with the surname of Anderson lived close to RAF Little Snoring, in a keeper's cottage in some woods adjacent to the airfield. Known for their hospitality, one evening in 1944 they hosted a dinner party and invited a young female WAAF Section Officer named Lucy Watson; a New Zealander by birth, she was based at nearby RAF Foulsham. Bertie was also invited to this dinner party and this chance meeting led to a blossoming relationship.

Lucy recalls,

> I was shy. I simply had to move to Little Snoring to be with him, I was determined. I was very junior to him; with dread and trepidation I went to his office. I knocked on his door. Thinking, I must get myself together, I walked in and I was immediately disarmed by the fact that he was leaning back on his chair with his feet on his desk looking rather casual. I stood there and managed to get the words out, that I wanted to move to Little Snoring. He agreed and I shot out of his office. I then realised this man was very important to me.

Lucy continues.

> My father had died, and Bertie, as the Station Commander, I had to ask his permission for me to take leave and attend the funeral. At the time I did not know him that well, but enough that he was very special to me! Of course, he gave me permission and said, 'I will take you to Harrogate, to the funeral, and fly you in my plane.' I was immensely happy with this outcome.

Lucy Hoare. (Courtesy of R. Russell)

As we were flying there it was virtually impossible to talk to one another with the aircraft engine noise. I started to feel very sick and I did not know what to do. I was desperate to impress him, I really did like him already the short time I had known him. I knew then I was going to be sick. I looked around for something to aid me in this task. The only item I could see was his cap. I whipped it off the seat and proceeded to be sick in it. I was mortified, I think he took it well, he was a very compassionate man.

Bertie wrote to his mother about the episode. 'This young woman had had a difficult life already, and I will take her to the funeral.' This statement was very true. Lucy's mother had suffered head injuries from a hunting accident and due to the wounds she sustained, she was placed in a nursing home in Scotland by Lucy's father; Lucy was told her mother had died. In fact, she survived until the early 1940s, and it was a terrible shock to Lucy to discover that her mother had been alive all these years.

Lucy recalled another occasion.

> One evening, Bertie invited me to a formal dance, we were dancing away in this beautiful ballroom dancing the Waltz, very close, all of a sudden my underwear went zoop down onto the floor, I stepped out of them. He bent down, picked them up and put them in his pocket and we carried out dancing. We did not miss a beat. I was vastly impressed!

Bertie told his mother he had always told Lucy he would not marry her while flying on Intruder operations as he believed he would not survive the war. Having beaten the odds at the end of hostilities, Bertie married Lucy Watson on 22 December 1945. After Bertie's untimely death in 1947, Lucy reflected with fond memories. 'I had married the perfect man and had a child, so why ever marry again!'

Above and opposite: Two photos of Bertie and Lucy on their wedding day. (Courtesy of T. Cushing)

L–R Bertie, Mrs Bessie Whitehead, and Lucy Hoare, at an official function. (Courtesy of T. Cushing)

Bertie later commented in a letter home regarding his wedding day:

HQAC SEAC
SEAC

Dearest Mummy,

How are things going? How are you and Lucy getting on, well? I don't seem to have written much. I cannot imagine her being anything but alright! But so, let me know exactly how she is.

I suspect you may have wondered after seeing all our troubles at Creek House before we were married, exactly how things are now, or rather were before I came out here. Well, I always meant to tell you in case it wasn't obvious, or was it? If it was, you will know that everything is perfectly alright, in fact nothing could be more perfect! I think our troubles were really due to the 'strung up us', and I have never been happier and I think Lucy is too. It is the most wonderful thing, and she really is the most wonderful person. All the doubts I had before the 22nd have completely gone. And nothing could possibly be better.

On the morning of the 22nd a sort of calm or peace came over me, this calm after the storms I suppose, complete happiness, it has lasted ever since. In fact, it has grown and grown. I suspect you could see this but I didn't want to tell you in case you couldn't. Still quite don't know where I am going, as I may not go to A.H.Q Malaya, but I will let you know as soon as I know myself. At present we are just on leave, enjoying ourselves very much. The other chaps are getting very weary waiting, but I like it, it's a complete rest and a chance, and doing me a lot of good. Sorry you had such a doo in the courts.

Bye bye all, love yours ever,
Rex

THE LOSS OF AN ACE

1946–47

Bertie was awarded a third MID on 1 January 1946. He attended Staff College at RAF Bracknell, Ramslade House, Berkshire, on 7 August for eight months. The college was under the command of Air Chief Marshal Sir Arthur Saunders.

On completion of his course at RAF Bracknell, Bertie was posted on 10 March 1946 to Headquarters Air Command, South East Asia Command (HQ, ACSEA), as an operations officer. Following the Japanese surrender in 1945, HQ, ACSEA had been transferred to Singapore, where it occupied several civilian buildings in Collyer Quay, from where it had direct control over all military stations and units on the island. The HQ moved from Collyer Quay to Changi in April 1946, and on 1 December 1946, when the command of the Far East was once again under British control after being led by a wartime Allied composition, the HQ, ACSEA was redesignated as Air Command, Far East (ACFE). This restructuring also abolished the post of Supreme Allied Commander, South East Asia, which was replaced by a Commander-in-Chief's Committee. With these changes, all new and existing Air Headquarters throughout the Far East, including AHQ Malaya, were brought under the aegis of the ACFE.

Now married, Lucy had joined Bertie in Singapore and, with the couple expecting their first child, they decided it was time for Bertie's heroic Air Force career to come to an end. He retired and accepted General Duties, gazetted in the *London Gazette* on 27 August 1946. With his desire to return to his love of farming, he decided he would retire from the RAF and they would both emigrate to Lucy's native country of New Zealand, where he would establish himself as a sheep farmer and live in peace and equanimity.

Above: RAF Bracknell, at Ramslade House, Berkshire. (Courtesy of Staff College, Shrivenham)

Right: Air Chief Marshal Sir Arthur Penrose Martyn Sanders GCB, KBE, RAF, was Commanding Officer of RAF Bracknell from 1945 to 1947. (Courtesy 12OCH)

Air Command, South East Asia Command (HQ, ACSEA), Headquarters, Collyer Quay, Singapore. (Courtesy Transpess)

After years of dicing with death, and the responsibility of command, he wanted to fade away into obscurity. However, he had one last mission to carry out.

Writing numerous letters home from Singapore, Bertie described how much Lucy and he were enjoying a quiet, tranquil life, away from the troubles of war and how Bertie's longstanding eye injury was still affecting him in life after his flying accident that had occurred many years before.

> There still seems to be lots of things I haven't told you about. My foot is of course quite okay now as you may have gathered from me playing tennis and things. My eye is really much the same, except the pupil does contract a little more with a bright light I suppose. I think that means I do see a little better, but very little. I do have a bit of trouble playing tennis as light is so bright on the courts. I have to wear dark glasses and they get misted up with sweat, and it is not as good as it should be. I am a bit thinner than I used to be, it seems the thin people get thinner, and fat ones get fatter out here! So will be a funny pair soon.

Lucy and Bertie, Singapore, 1946. (Courtesy of R. Russell)

Your venture into the world of make-up made me smile, will not know you when we come back. But what pity you have to revert to that sort of thing. Will have to come back and get you out into the country to put the roses back into your cheeks. We haven't now got the wireless set as we told you the battery not working. We can't have an electric one as we only have 110v current, that we make ourselves. Also, we only have the engine for few hours of darkness in the evenings. London BBC is not good out here anyway.

A letter from Lucy to Isabel, her mother-in-law, in February 1947:

We are flourishing and still enjoying the cool weather, the heat does not start until March or April, is there anything you would like for the house, mummy? Prices are falling gradually and one can get curtain material easily. Rex's eyes are still improving, and his shoulder rarely bothers him at all. He spends most of his off duty hours working on the boat and doing some carpentry. He wired all our house with electricity too, a very noble effort!

In mid-September 1946 the New Zealand government ordered a total of 80 ex-RAF Mosquito FB Mk VI aircraft from the Air Ministry, enough to re-equip three fully operational squadrons. In September 1946, the Air Ministry approved the sale of four training Mk III Mosquito aircraft, including spare engines, through the Commonwealth Disposals Commission at an individual price of £3,000 each aircraft. These aircraft, coded, A52-1015, A52-1003, A52-1005, and A52-1006, reached New Zealand shores on 7 November. A fifth aircraft, Mosquito FB Mk40, coded A52-101, arrived on 18 December – this aircraft beat the fastest crossing time across the Tasman sea by fifty minutes, a record originally held by Lieutenant John Kuver of the USAAF, who regularly flew B-25 Mitchells on courier flights, recording 5 hours and 4 minutes, later improved to 4 hours and 33 minutes by another USAF aircraft.

The remaining Mosquito aircraft that was ordered were flown to New Zealand from the UK, prepared at RAF Pershore, Worcestershire. They would be crewed by mixed RAF and RNZAF aircrews from No.1 Ferry

Inscribed on the back of the photograph reads. 'On our boat, rather a tangle I'm afraid.' (Courtesy of R. Russell)

Mosquito FB Mk VI, serial A52-101 coded SU-Z. (Courtesy of NZ Wings)

Unit, Transport Command. The first of these left England on 10 December 1946. The entire journey lasted three to four weeks, and a total distance of 11,800 miles were covered, with a total flying time of sixty hours, stopping at Tripoli, Lydda, Shaibah, Mauripur, Calcutta, Rangoon, Singapore, Perak, Darwin, and Sydney before reaching New Zealand.

Bertie saw this as a great opportunity to get back in the cockpit of his beloved Mossy! It was arranged that he would ferry one of these Mosquitos from Singapore to New Zealand, with Lucy following on, travelling via a Sunderland flying boat. In a letter to his mother of 12 February 1947, Bertie wrote:

> Where do you think we are going? To New Zealand! I may have told you that there are some Mosquitos being flown through to NZ and I have managed to get one of them to fly myself, and by the time you get this, should be there. Lucy is following in a Sunderland; we are going to stay with her numerous cousins. The address for mail will be C/O Mrs Watson, 10 Easedale

154

Street, Wellington, NZ. One cousin has a cabin on a lake for fishing which he is going to loan us.

The trip there, mine, goes through Sourabaya, the capital of Java, where there refuelled to Darwin for the night. Then Cloncurry in North Australia to Sydney where I will stay for a few days and look up some friends of mine, before going across to Wellington.

Mosquito fighter bomber Mk VI, serial TE746, destined for the RNZAF, departed the UK piloted by Flight Lieutenant John Field, carrying out numerous stops en route to refuel, before arriving at RAF Seletar, Singapore. Here the crew would swap with Bertie and Flying Officer Walter (Joe) Colvin, detached from 84 Squadron, who was reported as being very popular with his fellow squadron pilots. They would continue the final leg of the flight to New Zealand with frequent stops, across Australia. They departed RAF Seletar on 18 April 1947 en route to RAAF Darwin, stopping off at RAF Surabaya, Java for fuel.

When Mosquito TE746 landed at RAAF Darwin, on arrival Field reported a number of issues with the aircraft; the faults were reported to the engineering officer, Flying Officer Arthur Stephens, RAAF, who recalls:

> The leading edge of both mainplanes had been slightly damaged flying through heavy rain. This was repaired by doping strips of fabric along the leading edges and the wing tip edges and joints. The battery was recharged and one cracked cell in the battery was patched up with fabric and dope. A few U/S cockpit lamps were replaced.

What is of interest is the statement made by the flight engineering senior NCO, Flight Sergeant Charles Baker, RAAF, regarding the wireless set onboard the aircraft;

> When Mosquito TE746 landed at RAAF Darwin I was called on to service the W/T and R/T equipment. The pilot complained that prior to landing at DARWIN he was unable to make radio contact on any set. The W/T equipment included a T1154 Transmitter and a R1155 Receiver. R/T equipment

L–R Flight Lieutenant John Field and Lieutenant Walter Barton, SAAF, photographed at RAF Little Snoring in 1944 at a Station sports day. Field would fly Mosquito serial TE746 from the UK to RAF Seletar, Singapore. (Courtesy of T. Cushing)

was a TR5043, a new set being fitted here. After carrying out a ground test, it was found necessary to replace the VHF transceiver with a serviceable unit and also to calibrate the W/T transmitter.

Lucy writing from Singapore to her mother-in-law, explained the excitement of their impending move to New Zealand and starting their new life with their unborn daughter.

THE LOSS OF AN ACE

AHQ
MALAYA
SINGAPORE
23-3-47

Dearest Mummy,

The greatest news! I think that at last young Hoare is on the way, only a little way so far but all the signs & symptoms are there. Rex left for NZ some days ago and I imagine he is now in Sydney. It will be a grand trip for him, but I certainly do miss him! There is a faint hope that I might be able to follow him on Wednesday for a 3 week trip by air. Its somewhat unlikely though.

The small puppy we got some time ago has grown into a grand watch-dog. She sleeps under my bed and growls at every sound.

I am woken up at 06:30 am by a lump of dog jumping about on my tummy!

I do so hope this ghastly weather has cleaned up a bit.

The Telegraph have been held up recently, so we've been without news.

Hope the parcel arrived from Paddy safely?

All out love
Lucy

How is the house conversion going? It must be a dreadful struggle with these labour creatures.

At 09:08 on 26 March, Mosquito TE746, radio callsign 'Screwball 46', took off from RAAF Darwin, followed five minutes later by a second aircraft, TE927 piloted by Flight Lieutenant John Clark and Navigator Flying Officer Edwin Tippell (serial NZ 2330). Both aircraft steered a course of 112 degrees, with a transit altitude of 13,000ft en route for RAAF Garbutt, Townsville, Queensland, on the last leg of the journey, before going on to their final destination of New Zealand. Forty minutes into the journey Bertie reported that his R/T was unserviceable; his aircraft was last seen five or six miles on a parallel course. A severe tropical storm was reported over the Gulf of Carpentaria, and both aircraft were overdue their arrival time of

12:35 at RAAF Garbutt. However, shortly after 13:00, TE927 was reported to have successfully landed at Emergency Landing Ground Macrossan, Port Douglas. No sighting or radio communication was heard from Bertie's aircraft.

Clark later recalled details of the flight before losing contact with TE746:

> I made VHF contact with TE746 at approximately the position of 14'20S, 135'02'E, at about 09:45 hours, Darwin time. The Navigator replied that he was receiving me at strength 2 and that his W/T was U/S. I replied then I should call them again on crossing the coast, did so but received no reply. I left my VHF receiver on for a further 20 minutes but heard nothing more of TE746.

On landing at Macrossan, Clark contacted North Eastern Area HQ and informed the Senior Air Staff Officer, Wing Commander Bill Townsend, of the poor weather conditions and last known sighting of Mosquito TE927. Townsend later stated:

> At this time the weather had deteriorated over the whole of north Queensland to such an extent that all airfields in the Gulf country and Garbutt and adjacent airfields were closed. It was obvious that it was useless to attempt any air search that day, particularly as there was not a clue as to the missing aircraft's probable whereabouts. It was, therefore, decided to elicit as much information as possible from all available sources in order that a full appreciation could be made to assist in designing the future air search.

Mosquito TE746 was officially reported missing on 27 March, which initiated a search and rescue operation, supported by a C-47 Dakota, serial A65-35. However, this sortie was cancelled due to poor weather conditions. Townsend requested more aerial support and he was informed by HQ that a further three Liberators, A72-358, A72-365 and eventually A72-333, would join the search effort flying along the pre-planned flight path which Bertie had proposed to fly. They were unable to locate the downed Mosquito aircraft and were hampered further with poor weather conditions.

THE LOSS OF AN ACE

Lucy, against odds, had successfully made it to Australia and learned of the tragic news that her beloved husband was missing, recalling in a letter she wrote to her mother-in-law:

At Buckhurst
574 N.S Head Rd
Double Bay
Sidney
Sunday 30 March

My dearest Mummy,
You will by now have heard the news of Rex from Hermione. I sent it to her so that the shock might be broken more gently.

He left Singapore in his Mosquito in the greatest spirits on Thursday 20 March. There was bad weather all the way, and at Darwin consequently he did not get there until Wednesday 26. Weather still continued to be bad and he didn't arrive at Townsville, N. Australia scheduled on the same day.

Search parties couldn't get near the route he had taken for two days but yesterday the weather had cleaned up a bit.

They have found another missing Mosquito and tomorrow 12 a/c will cover the route he should have passed over.

They are all very hopeful of fine weather and of every success.

I was following him out to NZ by flying boat but am now waiting with relations in Sydney to be on the spot for further news.

God won't take him away Mummy I am sure they won't. You have suffered too much for this. We must only pray and hope, our faith will save him.

Mummy, I am so longing for you – it would help so much if we were together, perhaps before you get this I shall be able to cable you that all is well.

Will write Hermione, good night my dearest, sweetest mummy.

I only wish I could have held this from you, but I thought you would rather know to be with him in spirit.

God keep you safe and give you strength.
Lucy

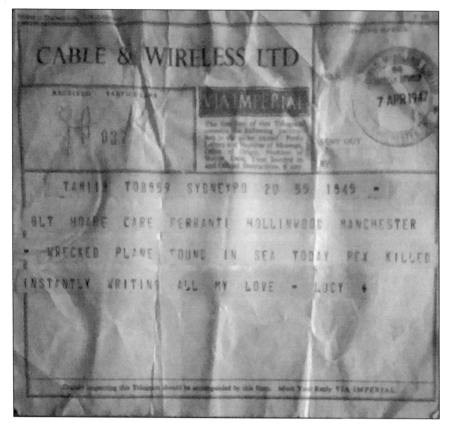

The telegram that Lucy sent to Hermione to give her the dreadful news her brother had been killed. (Courtesy of R. Russell)

The Mosquito that is remarked on in this letter was an RAAF reconnaissance mark of aircraft, flown by Flight Lieutenants Frank Longford and Douglas Batzoff. It crashed into Saddle Mountain, Cromarty, Australia, the wreckage was spotted by an Anson aircraft on 30 March and a ground party arrived the next day. Both crew were killed.

A close friend of Bertie's, Air Commodore Herbert George Brackley, wrote a letter to a mutual friend, commenting on the loss of Mosquito TE746:

> Unless Sammy and his Navigator bailed out, I should not give much for their chances of survival in a forced landing with a Mosquito between Darwin and Townsville. The country

between Normanton and Townsville is very thickly wooded for several hundred miles, and then the uplands become more open but very undulating but let us not give up hope. With Sammy's wonderful war record of day and night bad weather flying I cannot believe that the weather would beat him.

Search efforts continued; however, on the evening 3 April news was received that the flying doctor who ran the Missionary on Mornington Island, Reverend James McCarthy, had been told by locals that they had found an unknown wreckage. They had been travelling in a canoe and spotted the tail sticking up from a wrecked aircraft which was reported as, 'under water during these tides and was only visible at very low water' resting on a beach off Sydney Island, but they were too scared to get too close. The island was a small remote uninhabited island situated in the Gulf of Carpentaria, twenty miles off the Northern District of Queensland. At 09:30 on the morning of 4 April, a signal was sent to RAAF Cloncurry, Queensland, 300 miles away on the mainland by a Reuter Telegram from a 'pedal' wireless. The doctor instructed the locals to return to the crash site and mark it with some bed sheets that he provided, so a rescue aircraft

Air Commodore Herbert George Brackley, CBE, DSO, DSC. At the end of the war, he relinquished his commission and returned to the civilian airline world, initially as the Assistant to the Chairman of BOAC. Amongst his post-war achievements was the successful evacuation of 35,000 people from India to Pakistan following the partition of India. On 1 April 1948 he was appointed Chief Executive of British South American Airways Corporation. Tragically, on a stopover in Rio de Janeiro during a tour of South America, he drowned while swimming. (Courtesy of RAF web)

could easily locate the crash site. A rescue PBY-5A Catalina aircraft was immediately dispatched from No 114 ASR Flight, piloted by Flight Lieutenant Raymond Becke, who took off from RAAF Cloncurry to locate the crash site and find any survivors. On arrival Becke spotted the bed sheets that had been laid and then the wreckage of the downed Mosquito. Close by, two small inflated dinghies were floating in the water, but no sign of the crew. The Catalina flew low above the wreckage to identify any survivors, hoping that both downed airmen had bailed out or made it into the sea and paddled ashore and were somewhere sheltering on the island awaiting rescue. A rescue launch also set off from Mornington to assist with the rescue. Becke recalled what he saw when he arrived overhead at the crash site:

> I proceeded to Sydney Island and arrived over the island at 10:30 hours. I circled the island at a height of 500ft and sighted the wreckage about 200yds from the northern tip of Sydney Island. I made several runs over the wreckage at height of 50ft and identified the wreckage as that of an RAF Mosquito. I saw RAF markings and identified the tail unit as that of a Mosquito aircraft. I then signalled AORNWA and AORNEA reporting the finding of the wreckage and asked for further instructions. Before instructions were received, I had to return to Cloncurry to refuel. On landing, I received instructions from AORNWA to return to Sydney Island at first light on 5 April and, if possible, land on the water beside the wreckage and investigate.

Bertie's family, waiting at home in England, were praying for good news on the rescue efforts, and an atlas had remained open all the time on which his mother and sister attempted to picture with Air Force friends what might have happened following the updated information which had been received by the national newspapers. Bertie's mother is quoted in the *Daily Graphic* newspaper, dated 5 April:

> This is wonderful news. I had been told the chances were that he might have been blown some hundreds of miles off his course, and this fits in with the news tonight.

A RAAF PBY-5A Consolidated Catalina, similar to the aircraft that was flown by Flight Lieutenant Raymond Becke when he located the wreckage of Mosquito TE746. (Courtesy of adf-gallery)

Becke returned to the crash site as instructed but did not attempt a sea landing due to the proximity of reefs. However, he saw a number of people now at the crash site, including Reverend James McCarthy and Constable Thomas Richard Lugge, a local police officer from the island of Burketown.

Lugge stated:

> On Saturday the 5th April, I made a search of the wreckage of a crashed Mosquito aircraft at Sydney Island. I found parts of human body which appeared to be a left foot with toes. Black boy Lindsay of Mornington Island Mission found a small piece of shin bone apart six feet away from the wreckage. I made a thorough search of the wreckage; Mr J.B. McCarthy of Mornington Island Mission was present. Two unopened parachutes were taken from the wreckage. The wreckage was in tidal waters and was disintegrating due to the action of the tide. Lindsay saw a large shark quite close to the wreckage that morning, and there was numerous crabs in this area.

I am of the opinion that there were no more human remains at the scene of the crash. Natives from Mornington Mission searched Sydney Island and found no tracks of human beings. Five shoes two of one size, three of another were found washed ashore. A shirt and an officer's jacket, with one single stripe attached to each shoulder strap, were found washed ashore. The tide was rising and we were forced to discontinue the search. The wreckage is scattered over a large area of beach and bits of wreckage could be seen towards the sea. The tide here rises approximately seven feet and since the crash there has been considerable more flood water and in my opinion the wreckage will not last long there, it will be all washed away in a matter of a week or more and the engines will be the only signs available if they are not covered by mud and sand which is probable.

Becke confirms the series of events on arrival in the overhead of the crash site:

I arrived over Sydney Island at approximately 08:00 hours and on my arrival, I sighted six natives near the wreckage and two white men and three other natives walking towards the wreckage. I also sighted a launch five miles south-west of the wreckage. I circled the wreckage until the white men arrived at the wreckage, and while doing so I decided that I could not land the Catalina near wreckage because of the reefs. When the white men arrived at the wreckage, I dropped a message on paper from the aircraft asking if any human remains had been found, and if so to answer by writing on the sand 'Y' for Yes or 'N' for No. The answer to the message was 'Y' and beside this letter on the sand was a figure one, which I understood to mean one body had been found. Another message was dropped asking them would they be agreeable to convey the remains and any personal belongings left in the aircraft to the Mission Station at Mornington Island. I also added in the message that I would make a landing on Mornington Island strip and await the return of the launch.

Becke ascertained that they were agreeable to recover the human remains and personal belongings back to Mornington Island, so set a course for Mornington to await the ground party's return, landing there at 11:45, with the launch arriving at the Island at 18:45 the same day.

The crew of the Catalina stayed overnight at Mornington Island and prepared to take off on the morning of 6 April to return to Townsville. However, Catalina A24-111 became bogged down and was rendered unserviceable. Orders relayed to Becke that Catalina A24-114, of No 112 ASR Flight would arrive at the Island at 17:45, pick his crew and personal remains up, transport them to Townsville. Becke finally reached Townsville at 23:00 on 6 April, where he handed over the remains to the RAAF Medical Section and saw to it that the personal belongings were locked up in the guardroom cell. Among the personal effects was found an RAF blue tunic with the three braids on each sleeve afforded a Wing Commander, and the following ribbons: DSO and Bar, DFC and Bar, Mention in Dispatches, 1939–1945 Star, and an aircraft repeater compass.

Flight Lieutenant Thomas Thwaite, RAAF, a medical officer examined the remains of both crew members that were recovered, reporting his findings on 11 April:

> The said remains consisted of a human foot and attached distal third of leg. The integument had been stripped from underlying tissue and bone of Meta tarsus were partially disarticulated. Tibia was fractured in several places. State of decomposition of tissues would indicate that remains had been partially submerged in water for a period of seven to ten days.

The Hoare family received a letter, dated 10 June, from the Air Ministry detailing Bertie's tragic death, including a noteworthy statement: 'And that only remains, insufficient to establish identity, were recovered.'

A further letter dated 13 June from the Air Ministry concluded:

> The report from the Royal Air Force Mission to Australia states that, owing to the severity of the crash, it was not possible for the medical officer or the coroner at Townsville

to establish definitely the identity of the human remains recovered from the wrecked aircraft or, in the circumstance, to an issue a certificate of death. This unfortunate situation created a most unhappy difficulty in the matter of the burial arrangements and after consultation with the Royal Australian Air Force Headquarters it was decided that, when the Court of Inquiry had reached a decision on the deaths of both members of the crew, the remains should be enclosed in a leaden casket and dropped, with due honours, from an aircraft over the sea and that a memorial service should be held. This, it is understood, has now been done and the memorial service was held at St. Matthews Church, Townsville, Queensland, on Sunday, June 1st, the service being conducted by the Rev. J.G. Johnstone a former padre of the Royal Australian Air Force. The Department is advised that your daughter-in-law was interviewed by the Royal Australian Air Force representative in Sydney and informed of the reasons for the delay in the funeral arrangements and she is presumably in possession of all the sad details.

A subsequent Court of Inquiry were:

of the opinion that the pilot was not attempting a controlled landing, but that he, while flying through bad weather and unable to check his position because of unserviceability of wireless equipment, reduced height to base of cloud (50–100ft) to pinpoint his position and, in doing so, flew into the sea. … The crews were briefed by the Regional Flying Controller Officer, RAAF Darwin, he did not check instrument rating of pilot and therefore he failed in the performance of his duty in not complying with Air Board Order N.139/46 (Para.2), which states:

Any pilot who cannot produce certificate of rating will be classed 'not rated'.

And Para 7 (c) which states:

'Not rated' pilots may only be cleared for flights which are to be carried out completely in accordance with visual flight rules.

These are all contributing factors to the accident and loss of TE746, the weather was extremely poor and Bertie was flying the aircraft 'blind' and on instrument flight.

This search and rescue mission covered 250,000 miles and at the time was the largest search for a downed aircraft in Australian aviation history. This included numerous Liberator aircraft from RAAF Amberley and Ansons from RAAF Garbutt, and a Dakota C47 from RAAF Darwin.

A further recommendation made by Townsend was noting lack of appropriate survival equipment that was carried in these aircraft being ferried halfway across the world. Townsend himself understood the importance of being well equipped in such an eventuality, having been shot down in enemy occupied New Britain following a forced landing flying a Boston on 3 November 1943.

> These aircraft pass over some of the loneliest seas in the world and a considerable portion of the world's most primitive uninhabited terrain in which aircrews forced down without rations and water must surely perish. It has also been noted that these ferry crews do not wear suitable clothing for flights over such country. Where boots, gaiters, long sleeved shirts, and long trousers should be won, they are invariably attired in light clothing, light footwear, minus gaiters. Nor is any jungle kit as knives, maps, small medical gear etc, carried attached to the body.

Wing Commander Frederick Lambert (who had been squadron commander of 515 Squadron at RAF Little Snoring from January to December 1944) was working in the records department of the Air Ministry after the war. He recalls Bertie having kept a diary on scraps of paper when he was marooned next to his stricken aircraft. This diary was filed in his casualty record at the Air Ministry and records a tragic death.

Bertie's Navigator, Colvin, was killed outright. Bertie apparently broke both his legs, and due to the intense Pacific sun he could not withstand the heat of the cockpit, the Mosquito having a large glass canopy. Due to the severity of his injuries sustained in the crash, it is believed he fell from the wing of the aircraft, instantly collapsing onto

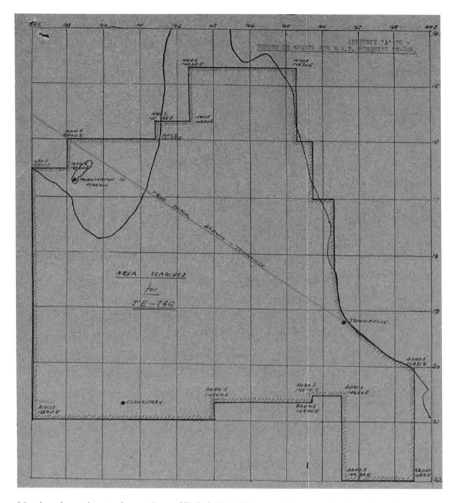

Navigation charts from the official RAAF casualty report showing the route that was flown by Mosquito TE746, and the extensive area that was covered by search and rescue aircraft, colours denoting each flight pattern. (Courtesy of NAA)

the sand bank below. Lambert mentions the scribbled last paragraph of the diary: 'being eaten alive, I cannot go on!' This specific area off Northern Australian was inhabited with Coconut Crabs, the largest species of the terrestrial hermit crab in the world. From this statement, along with the eyewitness account of Constable Thomas Lugge, further supported by absence of positive identification of both crew members, and only 'remains' of the latter being buried at sea in a leaden casket,

168

it is possible to conclude that Bertie and his Navigator met a very unpleasant end.

The official RAAF court of enquiry gives a similar outcome to the crews demise: 'Both members of the crew were killed and that the absence of bodies in wreckage was due to the presence of sharks in the area at wreckage.'

Many letters of condolence were sent to Bertie's sister, Hermione, sending support, she was devasted with the loss of her brother who she loved very much. Letters from family friends commenting:

> Wing Commander B.R.O.B Hoare, with his superb past record, and one of the 'finest types' now joins that happy band of pilots, of which he was one; with their endurance, skill and perseverance saved this small Island from destruction when the end seemed close at hand, and they gave their lives in so doing. There is a bond among pilots, which only pilots feel; our rather conceited conception of types is only a measure of what we think of ourselves, a sort of good type like me attitude.

Another letter addressed to Hermione on the loss of her brother:

> It is terribly hard to believe, Rex was one of the most alive people I knew, his vitality seemed to inspire one. He lived his life so, to the utmost of his power as all big men do. He made light of difficulties and his sight must have been an ever present difficulty to him, he 'marched breast forward', and now he has marched on into a fuller life and to you and your mother, a terrible blank, and to the country, the loss of a much needed leader of men.

A further letter of condolence sent to Bertie's mother, written by Pilot Officer Peter Morris, who had flown with Bertie as his Navigator when Bertie was serving as a Flight Commander and Squadron Commander of 23 Squadron in April 1942:

> Your son was one of the only few people whom I really respected during my time in the Royal Air Force. My last memory of

him was when he became CO of 23 Squadron. His leadership, unselfishness, and good fellowship was a permanent tonic to the squadron.

It had been my fond hope that we should meet again in the future, but as this cannot be, I am writing to you. I know that 'Sam' moved me writing sympathetic phrases, especially to you, so I will end by saying that many of us are sharing your loss.

If I may presume, I would like to suggest that you should be very proud to have been the mother of one whom I shall always respect and remember <u>as a truly gallant</u> British gentleman.

Yours Sincerely
Peter Boynes Morris

Bertie's ex-Commanding Officer, Wing Commander George Heycock, wrote to his mother, sending his sympathy for her loss:

GOC Heycock
Air H.Q
B.A.F.O
B.A.O.R

Dear Mrs Hoare,
It will be impossible to express how deeply Erith and I feel about Sammy, and what tremendous shock his accident was to us. To say nothing of the great loss he will be to the Air Force. We both, basically send our deepest sympathy and words are inadequate. But perhaps you may take comfort in the fact he has joined a gallant company of good friends.

With kindest regards and sincerely yours,
Bunty Heycock

The parents of the late Wing Commander Alan 'Sticky' Murphy also wrote to Bertie's mother. Alan was his close friend when they were based together

170

at RAF Little Snoring; he was killed in combat flying a Mosquito from RAF Little Snoring in 1944.

> My wife and I wish to contact you and show you our deepest and sincere sympathy in the loss of your gallant son. Our son, who was stationed with your son at Little Snoring, Wing Commander A.M. 'Sticky' Murphy, was killed on a flight over Holland, December 2, 1944. We very much treasure a letter of sympathy we had from your son at the time.
>
> Make god give you grace to bear this very great loss which you have sustained.
>
> > Kindest regards, and your very sincerely,
> > I. Murphy

Another letter received by Bertie's mother was from Mrs A Sherrington, the mother of Roy Sherrington, he was part of Bertie's crew in 1941 while serving with 23 Squadron:

> 'The Friary'
> 30 Lady Lane
> Chelmsford
> Essex
>
> 10.04.47
> Dear Mrs Hoare,
> I must apologise for troubling you, as I am sure you have had quite a number of letters in connection with your very sad loss.
>
> I am the mother of two very dear sons, both of whom have paid the supreme sacrifice and the younger one was with your son for a long time on various planes. His name was Roy (but I believe your son called him Sherry, short for surname). He was awarded the DFM while a navigator with Mr Hoare, I have very a nice photograph here of both, also his dogs and plane, probably you have one?

My son thought there was no one like your son, I know the feeling was mutual. Your son called here once, and he also knew my eldest son quite well. So, this is the reason I felt I must just send a line to say how deeply grieved we were to hear of Mr Hoare. A sad ending after such a wonderful life.

No one, only a mother knows exactly what a terrible blow it is and dear Mrs Hoare may I be allowed to express my heartfelt sympathy for you in your tremendous loss.

The one above can help us I am sure, for without that help I feel at times the loss would have been more than human strength could bear, and if I know you at all I am convinced you are doing your best to be brave as they would have wished us to be

So may God bless and comfort you and give you strength to carry on, hoping I have not taken a liberty in writing.

Yours in their dear names.
A.M Sherrington
PS My heart also goes out to his wife.

When the remains of both airmen were brought back to Townsville, Lucy was waiting for the sad news, recorded in a letter she wrote home:

At Buckhurst
574 N.S Head Rd
Double Bay
Sidney

Monday 7th April

My dearest mummy,
I still can't realise that he has moved to the higher life. It all seems so strange and impossible that he should go now after surviving, as one of God's chosen, the perils of a ghastly war. I begin to wonder if my faith is lacking, and this is a sort of punishment on me, but this does not make sense because you are made to suffer too.

He left Singapore in such gay spirits, delighted to be flying his beloved Mosquito again. They were killed on the day they left Darwin. The a/c crashed into the sea only about 100 yds from a small island in the Gulf of Carpentaria. They must have died instantly; the Mosquito was only sighted on Saturday half submerged in the sea. A native fisherman found it and told the flying doctor at a nearby island. An RAAF flying boat was sent out to bring them to Townsville where a military service will be held on Wednesday in the Cathedral there. Would you like a memorial service to be held in England mummy? We have the hymn in the church yesterday, 'Now above the skies he's king,' Rather wonderful wasn't it? I am now flying home as soon as possible can't get a passage until the end of May.

Lucy remained in Australia for a brief period of time, staying with the Australian media figure, Frank Packer; he had seen the death of Bertie in the world press in 1947 and that Lucy was alone in Australia. He immediately tracked her down and was adamant that she stayed with his family, while she was there, both Frank and his wife Gretel looked after her throughout her grieving. Pilot Officer Herbert James Bullmore, was Gretel's brother, he had served with Bertie in 1941–42 and always held him in high regard, as a friend and fellow Intruder

Sir Frank Packer, KBE, Australian media proprietor, 3 December 1906 – 1 May 1974. (Aus.media)

Pilot Officer Herbert James Bullmore, RAAF. He served with 23 Squadron in 1941/42, posted to Australia in June 1942 and posted to 22 Squadron RAAF. He was flying Boston A28-20, reported missing on 29 November between Port Moresby and Gona Mission to attack Japanese ground positions. The aircraft exploded as it released its ordnance of light fragmentation bombs, resulting in onboard explosions, with the aircraft crashing into shallow water just offshore. Due to this incident this type of bomb was not used again. Herbert is buried in Port Moresby War Cemetery, Papua New Guinea. His sister was Kerry Packer's mother. (Courtesy of Yorkshire Aircraft)

pilot. After the death of Herbert, Bertie made sure that his immediate family were supported. Packer also became godfather to Rosemary.

A service of remembrance was held on 25 April at 12:00 at St Thomas Church, close to the family home at d'Avigdor, Hove. A plaque was erected at St Mary and St Abram Church, also located close to the Hoare family home, its inscription reading:

> In proud remembrance of Bertie Rex O'Bryen Hoare, DSO DFC, Group Captain, RAF, Born 1912, Pioneer of the Intruders, Killed in flying duties March 26th, 1947, 'The Lord his Captain in the well fought fight.'

Rosemary Verity Hoare was born on 1 November 1947, but sadly never had the opportunity meet her father. (Courtesy of R. Russell)

Kranji War Cemetery, Singapore. (Courtesy of WW2 Cemeteries)

Both crew are remembered on the Memorial Roll of Honour at the Kranji War Cemetery, Singapore.

Lucy sadly died on 22 June 1970, aged 49 years, suffering from cancer. She was laid to rest at St Andrews Church, at Little Snoring, the place of which she was so fond. A service of remembrance was held, conducted by Canon Arthur Wylam, with many local villagers and ex-RAF personnel in attendance who knew and respected both Lucy and Bertie when serving at RAF Little Snoring together.

PERSONAL REFLECTIONS OF WING COMMANDER BERTIE HOARE

A Beautiful Aeroplane

Tommy Cushing was a young boy when the Second World War broke out, RAF Little Snoring was erected when he was away studying at boarding school. Returning home in late 1945, he recalls fond memories of the airfield and meeting Bertie in person.

> I was 8 years old at the time, it was just after the war, my father knew Bertie through a family called the Andersons. They were great entertainers who lived in the woods. I came to the airfield with father and my eldest brother, and Anderson. We came down to the HQ, I can remember a guard who was on a gate, in a little box near the entrance to the HQ. He went off to find Hoare, he came out and the guard came back and said follow that car. We came down and went to a hangar at the eastern end of the airfield. My brother climbed into the pilot's seat, which I felt a bit envious of, I got in the Navigators seat. While we were talking and looking around the plane, Bertie was talking to father and Anderson, he suddenly came up to the cockpit and looked up to me and said, 'what do you think of it?' I replied, 'you can't see out of it very well'. He said, 'oh yes you can, when it gets up level you can see out perfectly, beautiful aeroplane, beautiful!' Stroking his large handlebar moustache. Whenever Bertie went on leave my father would

take him to Norwich station, you think he would have his own driver to do that. He would telephone and say, 'I will be up at station in Norwich at a certain time', and my father would go and pick him up.

Tommy Cushing as a young boy, growing up living close to the airfield, witnessed RAF Little Snoring in its heyday. His father was close friends with Bertie. (Courtesy of T. Cushing)

Halifax NA259

Wing Commander Michael Renaut, Commanding Officer of 171 Squadron, recalled flying with Bertie when he took him up in a Mosquito on 26 June 1945.

> One of my Halifax crews was showing off low flying over the beach at Cromer when it crashed. The pilot was evidently approaching the beach from seawards and 'beating up' the crowds on the beach. On the second run, at high speed, he failed to pull the aircraft up over the cliffs and flew straight onto the cliff face – it may have been the effect of a strong breeze causing peculiar air currents. The Halifax exploded and burning pieces showered bathers on the sands below and eighteen people were killed. I felt most annoyed as squadron commander that a crew who had survived the war should kill themselves in the way and I felt most upset at having to write unnecessary letters of sympathy to relatives. Group Captain Sammy Hoare, who commanded the Mosquito station at Little Snoring, flew over to North Creake in his Mosquito as he'd promised to let me fly it. I took over control when we were airborne and flew along to Cromer to see the wreckage of my Halifax from the air and later landed the Mosquito. It was a lovely aeroplane to fly and so light and sensitive after the lumbering Halifax. I got used to it very easily and wished that I'd flown them more.

Halifax NA259 was piloted by Warrant Officer Ian Wilshire Dent, Royal Australian Air Force, with a full complement of a crew of three onboard. They off from RAF North Creake, Norfolk, at 14:58 on 25 June conducting an Air Test. Airborne for ten minutes the aircraft was seen to turn towards Cromer Cliffs at 1,000ft. Eyewitnesses believe the pilot, Dent, was having engine trouble and looked as if he was going to make a force landing on the beach. All the aircraft's engines throttled back and smoke was seen to be omitting from both outer engines. Dent saw how many people were on the beach and pulled off his approach last minute. The wing tip struck the cliffs and the stricken bomber burst into flames, the wreckage settling at the

A birdseye view of RAF crash recovery teams removing wreckage of Halifax III NA259 from Cromer beach. Due to the difficult location, fire crews were lowered down by rope to the site. It took over an hour to distinguish the flames. (Courtesy of Aircrew Remembered)

foot of the cliffs, all crew were killed. There were civilian casualties who were close to the crash, including a USAAF Sergeant Gleddening and his English wife; they were on the beach at the time and were taken to Cromer Hospital for treatment of shock and minor burns. After the incident, a court of enquiry found that Dent had disregarded his briefing that day by his Flight Commander, who was also disciplined for poor supervision.

The other crew members were:
    Navigator: Sergeant William Way
    Flight Engineer: Sergeant Raymond Ernest George Seymour
    Air Gunner: Sergeant Andrew Mill Adams

Posted out the Squadron with a DFC

Flying Officer Douglas Badly, nicknamed 'Bud', originally from New Zealand was serving with 23 Squadron at RAF Little Snoring in 1944 flying Mosquitos. He had a remarkably successful career as an operational pilot but crossed Bertie's path more than once, he recalls: 'It was a squadron reunion at the officers' mess, there was an unserious photograph and then a serious one being taken.'

Douglas decided to raise his sherry glass for the serious photograph at a height that appeared to show it perched on the Station Commander's head. Bertie was not amused with the outcome!

> He was furious, he said, we had the serious photograph and I ruined it by putting that glass above his head. Telling my CO, Wing Commander Murphy he wanted me kicked off the Squadron. Him turning around and saying he could not do that as I was one of his most experienced pilots. He never forgot though, as the CO was killed on 2 December and I was posted out on 3 December.

Another occasion that he recalls with humour, was on the 26 September 1944, flying as No.2 in Mosquito *Z-Zebra,* with his Navigator, Flight Sergeant Alex Wilson. His lead was Flying Officers George Stewart and

Flying Officer Douglas 'Bud' Badly standing second row, sixth from the left. (Courtesy of T. Cushing)

2 photographs taken of a 23 Squadron reunion at RAF Little Snoring, 1944. Group Captain Hoare is seated front centre, seated second from his left is Wing Commander Alan Michael 'Sticky' Murphy, CO 23 squadron, he was killed on a Mosquito Intruder operation on the night of 2 December 1944, over Zwolle, Netherlands. Note, on the formal photograph the glass perched above Bertie's head, deliberately placed there by Flying Officer Douglas 'Bud' Badly. (Courtesy of T. Cushing)

Navigator Paul Beaudet in Mosquito *T-Tare*. Both aircraft were returning from a successful Day Ranger mission over Denmark having engaged ground targets at a Luftwaffe airfield at Grove. They returned over the Danish coast and saw an opportunity target. Pretty shot up as a result, Douglas managed to reach RAF Woodbridge, Suffolk, on only one engine and safely landed his aircraft.

> I was attacking a Freya radar on the coast, there was one chap standing there with a machine gun pistol, he knocked my engine out and I couldn't use the elevator, the only way I could go up and down was on the trim tab. My new Navigator, as my old one had completed his tour of duty. I said, 'you will have to bail out'. He could not bail out as he pulled his parachute rip cord by mistake and I had silk everywhere. I tried to fly the aeroplane on one engine, trim it and had all this silk in front of me. It took us nearly 3 hours, a long trip! When we got back, I managed to land it alright, I rang up the station, unfortunately

> Group Captain Hoare answered the telephone. I asked him if he could send an aeroplane to pick us up. He replied, 'No I bloody can't, you can come back on the train'. So, there was me and my Navigator with our parachutes and navigational kit struggling on this train. I got on the train and could not believe it, my girlfriend, Shelia was up the other end of the carriage. She was shouting and cursing at me saying I had done enough Ops.

It did not end there for him: when he finally got back to RAF Little Snoring he was called to Station Headquarters and to see Bertie.

> I got told off about one of his aeroplanes being down at RAF Woodbridge, I went off a bit feeling a bit glum, an hour later I got called back into his office and he congratulated me for getting an instant DFC, I guess I ended better up in the end.

Badly later found out Air Vice-Marshal Edward Addison, Air Officer commanding 100 Group, had read his combat report at HQ and said he had showed brilliant skill and should be awarded an 'immediate' DFC.

Flying Officer George Stewart's personal account supports the skilled actions of his No.2 that day:

> At the coast, I took a pass at a Freya with cannons and machine guns, remembering those many times we had been scanned by them at night, in our intruder patrols. As I passed overhead, I saw a machine gun nest, and heard a small bullet came in past Paul's shoulder and hit the base of the starboard feathering button. I straightened out heading home. Bud was hit severely, as he followed me in my attack, he lost one engine, rudder, and elevator control, but miraculously recovered control. Just barely over the water and brought it home, it was a stroke of genius that he accomplished it. I radioed Bud, but no reply, and as there was cloud all around, I couldn't have found him. I landed back at Little Snoring, when ages later this 'Thing' came flying at a crazy angle flew overhead. It was Bud, who carried onto Woodbridge to land safely. 'Sammy' Hoare was furious and cancelled all such trips in the future.

Above and left: Footage from Flying Officer George Stewart's Mosquito aircraft gun camera, flying at an extremely low altitude engaging the Freya radar. This radar was a Wassermann M II, Serial No.1268 located at radar station Ringelnatter in Northern Houvig, Denmark. Built on a sand dune with supporting accommodation and office fortifications, only slight damage was caused by the attack with a few cables shot through, which were repaired. With recalibration of the radar head, it was operational in a few days. (Courtesy of T. Cushing)

Above: Flying Officer Douglas 'Buddy' Badly standing with Bessie Whitehead, he was engaged to her daughter at the time, Shelia Whitehead, known as the blue-eyed blonde of Little Snoring village. (Courtesy of T. Cushing)

Right: Shelia Whitehead remembers Bertie in 1945. 'Sammy Hoare is still a bugger as ever. He makes everyone do parades at 08:50 each morning, his Air Crew too! This is in order that he can put up a good show on VE Day.' (Courtesy of T. Cushing)

The Officers' Mess Garden

As Station Commander at RAF Little Snoring Bertie was a keen gardener, living in a small annex off an RAF hut located in the centre of Little Snoring village that he had built when he arrived at the station. Bertie lived on one side of the building, and in the other half lived Wing Commander Alan 'Sticky' Murphy, Commanding Officer 23 Squadron – which was strange because he was married.

Also a keen game shooter, Bertie thought by becoming friends with the local dignitaries and landowners it would aid him getting their permission to shoot on the surrounding fields adjacent to the airfield. He decided to hold a social function in the Officers' Mess one Sunday afternoon; a new 'rustic' style fence was erected, and a lush grass lawn was laid. This fence provided an excellent 'perch' to lean bicycles against. Late one evening in the nearby town of Fakenham, a merry group of 23 Squadron pilots were returning from the pub, home to RAF Little Snoring. Squeezed into one car, they stopped close to the airfield. They had stumbled across two public works

L–R Pilot Officers Fred Bocock, Arthur Harvey, Flight Lieutenant Bill Gregory, and Squadron Leader John Tweedale relaxing outside the Officers' Mess at RAF Little Snoring. Behind them can be seen the fence that was demolished after the pilots' 'rowdy' night out. (Courtesy of T. Cushing)

A Nissen Hut located on the South-West corner of RAF Little Snoring, Bertie lived on one side, with Wing Commander Alan Michael 'Sticky' Murphy, Commanding Officer 23 Squadron on the other, a small garden was tended by both senior officers. (Courtesy of T. Cushing)

traction engines that had been used to repair the nearby road, described by one of the crowd as 'gently breathing away', having had their fires lit earlier and slowly dying out. To the amazement of all the group, they got these beasts rolling free and slowly moving. One stopped, but the other one marched forward and made its way back to camp – headed straight towards the Officers' Mess! The driver of this contraption did not know how to stop it, or had overlooked that part, as it continued straight over the freshly cut grass and into the fence. Described by one pilot with hilarity, 'the lawn sank quite a few inches and this beast stopped at the steps to our front door. Maybe it did not have enough steam to climb up the steps.'

Next morning found Bertie standing, looking at the sight of his now demolished rustic fence, with bicycle handlebars and bells sticking up out from the sunken lawn, to add an indented steam roller, he was certainly not amused.

A photograph taken on the lawn of the Officers' Mess of RAF Little Snoring HQ Flight. Bertie can be seen front and centre with Squadron Leader Bob Muir, his Navigator seated third from right on the same row. (Courtesy of T. Cushing)

Right: Flying Officer George
Stewart. (Courtesy of
100 Group Association)

Below: Flying Officers Paul
Beaudet and George Stewart,
photographed in June 1944.
(Courtesy of World Press)

Flying Officers George Stewart and Paul Beaudet photographed next to their Mosquito. (Courtesy of World Press)

ANNEXES

Operational Flying Record Log

Date	A/C Type	Serial	(Exact Times) T/O / Landing	Remarks
			1941	
20 Feb	Blenheim I	YP-B	21:40 / 00:25	Intruder Ops
03 Mar	Blenheim I	YP-T	22:30 / 00:30	Intruder Ops
08 Mar	Blenheim I	YP-T	22:10 / 00:50	Intruder Ops
11 Mar	Blenheim I	YP-T	22:20 / 01:15	Intruder Ops
12 Mar	Blenheim I	YP-T	23:40 / 02:10	Intruder Ops
08 Apr	Blenheim I	YP-T	23:00 / 01:30	Offensive Patrol
09 Apr	Blenheim I	YP-T	00:10 / 02:40	Offensive Patrol
15 Apr	Blenheim I	YP-N	03:50 / 05:30	Offensive Patrol
17 Apr	Blenheim I	YP-H	22:35 / 00:55	Offensive Patrol
21 Apr	Blenheim I	YP-T	21:30 / 23:59	Offensive Patrol
28 Apr	Havoc I	YP-D	00:25 / 02:45	Offensive Patrol
02 May	Havoc I	YP-D	01:00 / 03:15	Offensive Patrol
03 May	Havoc I	YP-D	00:15 / 04:25	Offensive Patrol
06 May	Havoc I	YP-D	01:49 / 04:40	Offensive Patrol
07 May	Havoc I	YP-D	02:05 / 04:45	Offensive Patrol
10 May	Havoc I	YP-D	00:55 / 03:13	Offensive Patrol
11 May	Havoc I	YP-B	03:00 / 05:00	Offensive Patrol

Date	A/C Type	Serial	(Exact Times) T/O / Landing	Remarks
11 Jun	Havoc I	YP-T	01:15 / 04:05	Offensive Patrol
15 Jun	Havoc I	YP-X	02:45 / 04:00	Offensive Patrol
16 Jun	Havoc I	Unk	Unk	Offensive Patrol
24 Jun	Havoc I	YP-B	00:10 / 03:40	Offensive Patrol
01 Jul	Havoc I	YP-T	01:40 / 03:30	Offensive Patrol
06 Jul	Havoc I	YP-T	01:50 / 04:10	Offensive Patrol
08 Jul	Havoc I	YP-T	01:40 / 03:10	Offensive Patrol
13 Jul	Havoc I	YP-T	02:00 / 04:00	Offensive Patrol
17 Jul	Havoc I	YP-H	01:30 / 01:50	Aborted
21 Jul	Havoc I	YP-T	01:30 / 04:10	Offensive Patrol
22 Aug	Havoc I	YP-T	22:00 / 00:15	Offensive Ops
26 Aug	Havoc I	YP-J	01:30 / 03:30	Offensive Ops
28 Aug	Havoc I	YP-P	23:45 / 01:50	Offensive Ops
30 Aug	Havoc I	YP-K	02:25 / 04:25	Offensive Ops
07 Sep	Havoc I	YP-L	03:20 / 05:10	Offensive Ops
13 Sep	Havoc I	YP-A	21:15 / 23:40	Offensive Ops
20 Sep	Havoc I	YP-T	22:10 / 22:35	Aborted
23 Oct	Havoc I	YP-T	01:15 / 02:15	Unk
15 Nov	Havoc I	YP-J	21:10 / 23:55	Offensive Ops
28 Dec	Havoc I	Unk	20:18 / 22:26	Offensive Ops
1942				
28 Jan	Havoc I	YP-U	02:55 / 05:20	Offensive Ops
11 Feb	Boston III	Unk	21:13 / 23:05	Intruder Ops
24 Feb	Boston III	Unk	23:45 / 01:35	Intruder Ops
01 Mar	Boston III	Unk	00:47 / 03:15	Intruder Ops
09 Mar	Boston III	Unk	02:55 / 04:55	Intruder Ops
24 Mar	Boston III	Unk	22:00 / 00:40	Intruder Ops

Date	A/C Type	Serial	(Exact Times) T/O / Landing	Remarks
26 Mar	Boston III	Unk	00:25 / 02:58	Intruder Ops
01 Apr	Boston III	Unk	23:43 / 01:43	Intruder Ops
02 Apr	Boston III	Unk	22:11 / 01:00	Intruder Ops
03 Apr	Boston III	Unk	20:28 / 22:30	Intruder Ops
10 Apr	Boston III	Unk	21:43 / 00:43	Intruder Ops
14 Apr	Boston III	Unk	02:25 / 04:45	Intruder Ops
16 Apr	Boston III	Unk	01:25 / 04:25	Intruder Ops
26 Apr	Boston III	Unk	22:25 / 00:15	Intruder Ops
03 May	Boston III	YP-W	22:30 / 01:40	Intruder Ops
07 May	Boston III	YP-C	22:45 / Unk	Intruder Ops
28 May	Boston III	YP-H	00:55 / 04:05	Intruder Ops
30 May	Boston III	YP-H	22:35 / 01:46	Intruder Ops
31 May	Boston III	YP-H	01:35 / 04:00	Intruder Ops
01 Jun	Boston III	Unk	Unk	Intruder Ops
04 Jun	Boston III	Unk	Unk	Intruder Ops
07 Jun	Boston III	Unk	Unk	Intruder Ops
08 Jun	Boston III	Unk	Unk	Intruder Ops
17 Jun	Boston III	Unk	Unk	Intruder Ops
22 Jun	Boston III	Unk	Unk	Intruder Ops
23 Jun	Boston III	Unk	Unk	Intruder Ops
24 Jun	Boston III	Unk	Unk	Intruder Ops
25 Jun	Boston III	Unk	Unk	Intruder Ops
27 Jun	Boston III	Unk	Unk	Intruder Ops
05 Jul	Mosquito II	YP-S	02:23 / 04:30	Intruder Ops
06 Jul	Mosquito II	YP-S	00:10 / 03:10	Intruder Ops
11 Jul	Mosquito II	YP-B	23:42 / 03:10	Intruder Ops
12 Jul	Mosquito II	YP-B	01:12 / 03:55	Intruder Ops

Date	A/C Type	Serial	(Exact Times) T/O / Landing	Remarks
21 Jul -	Mosquito II	YP-E	02:00 / 04:08	Intruder Ops
23 Jul	Mosquito II	Unk	Unk	Intruder Ops
28 Jul	Mosquito II	YP-B	02:15 / 04:38	Intruder Ops
30 Jul	Mosquito II	YP-B	00:10 / 03:35	Intruder Ops
01 Aug	Mosquito II	YP-B	00:33 / 03:08	Intruder Ops
02 Sep	Mosquito II	YP-L	21:25 / 00:50	Intruder Ops
06 Sep	Mosquito II	YP-B	21:22 / 00:45	Intruder Ops
10 Sep	Mosquito II	YP-B	Unk / 00:26	Intruder Ops
13 Sep	Mosquito II	YP-B	01:35 / 03:10	Intruder Ops
24 Sep	Mosquito II	YP-R	00:28 / 01:49	Intruder Ops
1943				
23 Sep	Mosquito VI	UP-E	23:10 / 02:00	Intruder Ops
27 Sep	Mosquito VI	UP-L	20:46 / 01:30	Intruder Ops
02 Oct	Mosquito VI	UP-L	21:10 / 02:20	Intruder Ops
07 Oct	Mosquito VI	UP-L	21:57 / 00:50	Intruder Ops
08 Oct	Mosquito VI	UP-L	00:29 / 04:50	Intruder Ops
20 Oct	Mosquito VI	UP-L	22:05 / 01:30	Intruder Ops
03 Nov	Mosquito VI	UP-L	19:14 / 22:35	Intruder Ops
10 Nov	Mosquito VI	UP-U	01:46 / 04:30	Intruder Ops
03 Dec	Mosquito VI	UP-L	03:50 / 05:20	Intruder Ops
10 Dec	Mosquito VI	UP-L	19:33 / 22:25	Intruder Ops
19 Dec	Unk		Unk	Transit Flight
20 Dec	Mosquito VI	UP-L	21:04 / 23:30	Intruder Ops
1944				
02 Jan	Mosquito VI	UP-L	02:06 / 07:31	Intruder Ops
04 Jan	Mosquito VI	UP-L	20:23 / 23:23	Intruder Ops
10 Jan	Mosquito VI	UP-L	02:27 / 04:43	Intruder Ops

Date	A/C Type	Serial	(Exact Times) T/O / Landing	Remarks
14 Jan	Mosquito VI	UP-L	18:53 / 23:08	Flower Patrol
21 Jan	Mosquito VI	UP-L	21:31 / 02:32	Flower Patrol
03 Feb	Mosquito VI	UP-L	20:10 / 00:04	Night Ranger
04 Feb	Mosquito VI	UP-L	05:30 / Unk	Intruder Patrol
11 Feb	Mosquito VI	UP-L	20:30 / 23:00	Intruder Patrol
19 Feb	Mosquito VI	UP-L	01:02 / 04:03	Flower Patrol
20 Feb	Mosquito VI	UP-L	22:44 / 01:05	Intruder Patrol
23 Feb	Mosquito VI	UP-L	18:48 / 21:56	Intruder Patrol
24 Feb	Mosquito VI	UP-L	22:49 / 01:03	Flower Patrol
07 Mar	Mosquito VI	UP-L	21:31 / 01:06	Flower Patrol
14 Mar	Mosquito VI	UP-L	23:00 / 02:20	Intruder Patrol
15 Mar	Mosquito VI	UP-L	21:25 / 01:40	Flower Patrol
22 Mar	Mosquito VI	UP-L	21:45 / 00:21	Flower Patrol
23 Mar	Mosquito VI	UP-L	20:08 / 23:42	Intruder Patrol
24 Mar	Mosquito VI	UP-L	20:50 / 02:25	Flower Patrol
05 Jul	Mosquito VI	YP-B	00:20 / 03:45	Intruder Patrol
10 Jul	Mosquito VI	YP-B	17:35 / 20:35	Intruder Patrol
05 Aug	Mosquito VI	YP-B	14:00 / 16:00	Aborted
09 Aug	Mosquito VI	YP-B	01:20 / 05:10	Intruder Patrol
11 Aug	Mosquito VI	YP-B	13:15 / 18:35	Escort Duties
29 Aug	Mosquito VI	YP-B	00:45 / 06:00	Intruder Patrol
04 Sep	Mosquito VI	YP-B	21:30 / 04:00	Intruder Patrol
22 Oct	Mosquito VI	YP-B	15:40 / Unk	Transit Flight
28 Dec	Mosquito VI	YP-B	20:02 / 00:25	Ranger Patrol
1945				
22 Feb	Mosquito VI	548	20:30 / 00:45	Ranger Patrol
25 Feb	Mosquito VI	548	15:29 / 16:55	Aborted
23 Mar	Mosquito VI	548	21:10 / 01:35	Intruder Ops

Combat Claims

* This information has been amended to show correct data, a majority of these claims cannot be confirmed without the appropriate Luftwaffe records which have been destroyed or lost over time.

Date	Type	Result
1941		
03 Mar	1x Unk E/A	Damaged
09/10 Apr	1x Convoy	Destroyed
21 Apr	1x Ju 88*	Destroyed
03/04 May	1x He 111	Destroyed
	1x Ju 88	Probable
07 May	1x Unk E/A	Probable
11 May	1x Unk E/A	Damaged
16 Jun	2x Runway beacons	Destroyed
13 Sep	1x He 111	Destroyed
	1x He 111*	Damaged
28 Dec	Marshalling yard	Damaged
1942		
09 Mar	Marshalling yard	Damaged
26 Mar	Ground Positions	Unk
01/02 Apr	Marshalling yard	Unk
03 Apr	Factory	Destroyed
03 Apr	2x Unk E/A	Damaged
16 Apr	Airfield	Damaged
26 Apr	Airfield	Damaged
28 May	1x Unk E/A	Probable
28/29 May	1x Locomotive	Damaged
30/31 May	Airfield	Unk
31 May/01 Jun	Marshalling yard	Damaged

Date	Type	Result
01 Jun	Airfield	Damaged
01 Jun	1x Locomotive	Damaged
08 Jun	Marshalling yard	Damaged
06/07 Jul	1x Do217	Destroyed
30/31 Jul	1x Fw200 Condor*	Destroyed
10 Sep	1x Unk E/A	Destroyed
1943		
27/28 Sep	Bf110*	Destroyed
07 Oct	1x Unk E/A	Unk
08/09 Oct	1x Unk E/A	Unk
	Airfield	Unk
10/11 Nov	1x Locomotive	Damaged
10 Dec	1x Do217	Unk
1944		
10/11 Jan	1x Ju188	Destroyed
21/22 Jan	1x Unk E/A	Damaged
03 Feb	1x Unk E/A	Damaged
03 Feb	1x Unk E/A	Probable
20/21 Feb	1x Unk E/A	Damaged
14/15 Mar	1x Locomotive	Damaged
24/25 Mar	1x Me 109*	Destroyed
05/06 Jul	1x Locomotive	Damaged
29/30 Aug	2x Unk E/A	Damaged
03/04 Sep	6x Unk E/A	Damaged
1945		
22 Mar	1x Locomotive	Damaged
22 Mar	2x Convoy	Destroyed
22 Mar	1x Convoy	Damaged
23/24 Mar	Airfield	Damaged

Physical Training in Blackout Conditions

An official RAF report was commented on by Group Captain Rupert Henry Archibald Leigh, commanding officer of RAF Charter Hall, Berwickshire, relating to his personal opinion on physical training in the rare situation being found in Blackout conditions. It was forwarded to Bertie when he was officer commanding at 60 OTU. They had served together in 23 Squadron in 1941, when Leigh was the Commanding Officer between May–December 1941.

Leigh was also a good friend of Group Captain Douglas Bader and was given the task of conducting Bader's test flight when Bader was given the clearance by the Central Medical Establishment. Conducting a test flight in a Harvard aircraft, equipped with toe brakes which Bader would be unable to operate with his artificial legs, Leigh operated these knowing that on operations Bader would be flying Spitfires and Hurricanes which were fitted with hand operated brakes.

FORTHCOMING WEDDING

Miss Helen Brenda Smith, only daughter of Mr and Mrs J. Herbert Smith, Whincrag, Newport, Fife, and Flying Officer Rupert H. A. Leigh, youngest son of Judge and Mrs Leigh, Riversdale, Wilmslow, Cheshire, whose wedding will take place at St Thomas's Church, Newport, on 4th August.

A newspaper article, August 1942. (Courtesy of BBHS)

GRADED TABLES FOR 6 WEEK COURSE
Table 1. Introductory Table
Exercises
(a) Walking round room in line, hands on shoulders of man in front.
(b) Running round room in some formation.
(c) Walking freely – avoiding people and objects.
(d) Skip jumping on the spot, down to crouch on the fifth count.
(e) Game – Find the white hoop.
(f) Walking down centre of room, finding the skittles and counting them aloud.
(g) Walking Relay – with skittle.

Table 2
(a) Walking freely – avoiding people and objects.
(b) Running freely – avoiding obstacles.
(c) Hop and swing exercise.
(d) Game – Find the ball.
(e) Run to find edges of wall painted white. (Last one to do so given three press-ups).
(f) Straddle jump.
(g) Walking towards certain defined objects.

Table 3
(a) Walking freely – giants and dwarfs avoiding obstacles.
(b) Partners facing – 10 yards apart. Run to touch partner (astride) through his legs and back to place.
(c) Knee stretching from crouch position.
(d) Game   (1) Avoid the bean bags.
         (2) Collecting as many bean bags as possible within a specified time.
(e) Knee Boxing in pairs.
(f) Hopping over Benches.
(g) Throwing bean bags into hoops on the ground.

BALL TRAINING
Table 4
(a) In circle formation – passing the ball from hand to hand then short distances apart.
(b) Tower Ball.

(c) Arch Relays.
(d) Ball Passing – in partners.
(e) 'Scotch' Handball.
(f) Jockeys and Riders with ball.
(g) Dual Relay with ball.

BALANCE TRAINING
Table 5
(a) Hopping avoiding obstacles.
(b) Balance Bench exercises.
(c) Ball passing in pairs on one foot.
(d) Hopping from hoop to hoop.
(e) Distance touch.
(f) Round the thumb – balance walk.
(g) Team circle walking-on whistle – Balance.

REVISION TABLE
Table 6
Revision of work done –
Exercises –
(a) Walking and running avoiding obstacles.
(b) Relay Races.
(c) Balance Exercises.
(d) Ball Training.
(e) Target Practice.

His response ……

CONFIDENTIAL
From:- Officer Commanding R.A.F Station, Charter Hall
To:- No.60 OTU (For the attention of G/C A.G. Miller, DFC, O.L)
Date:- 27 July 1943.
Ref:- CH/RHAL/DO.

PHYSICAL TRANING IN BLACKOUT CONDITIONS
With reference to Headquarters, No 9 Group letter 9G/S.1320/13/Trg, dated 21st July 1943, on the above subject, considerable difficulty has been experienced at this Unit with some of the minutiae of the agenda:

Table 1. Exercise

(c). A number of people at this OTU experience difficulty in avoiding people and objects in broad daylight and, therefore, it is felt that there is little need to complicate matters.

(d). Normally we have a minimum of 30 pupils exercising at one time, and experience has shown that the spot has to be a large one.

It is universally felt that the somewhat complicated process of getting down to crouch on the fifth count is not entirely devoid of charm and exhilaration.

(e). We have stopped playing this game since a Dominion member of aircrew detailed to hide the white hoop exercises a little too much initiative and ingenuity.

(f). What about the beer?

(g). This of course is considerably more difficult than without the skittles.

Table 2. Exercise

(c). We cannot perform the exercise realistically owing to the absence without leave of our band, but we have gramophone recitals every Wednesday evening at 8 o'clock.

(e). After a very little time it was found that all personnel could find their way to the bars blindfolded. In this connection we are sanguine that the word 'press-ups' is a typist's error.

(f). This exercise was going fine until someone turned the lights on.

(g). A number of Officers apparently confused this exercise with (e) supra.

Table 3. Exercise

(a). This is not understood.

(b). After representation from the local Watch Committee, we were reluctantly compelled to abandon this age-old exercise.

(c). Tres rare et curieux.

(d). I have spoken to the Padre and he quite agrees that the avoidance of bean bags is very necessary to the welfare of modern civilisation. In this connection, we have stopped flying for two days in order that all personnel may go out and gather as many bean bags as possible.

(e). This entertaining little exercise originated in a place called Borneo. You may remember that a horrid madman came from those parts who, I am told, had huge warts on his knees. It was found that by learning to box with the knees (in blackout) the evil intentions of this sinister old man could be thwarted.

Table 3. Exercise

(f). From this exercise we go by easy stages to the even simpler exercise of hopping over a cliff.

(g). We tried this exercise for some time but unfortunately, owing to the darkness, it was difficult to distinguish between hoops and bean bags, with the result that there were some claims under the Workman's Compensation Act (1925).

Table 4

(a). It was found impracticable to persevere with the harsh and painful exercise.

(b). None are held on the station, but they have been (c) indented for.

(d). I do not think I understand this exercise. Furthermore, I do not think I want to.

(e). This exercise has placed us in something of a quandary. We have all, of course, heard of 'Scotch Whitecocks' and a number of us have consumed 'Rye Highballs', but what a 'Scotch Handball' is we are not certain. After no small deliberation, we have come to the conclusion that the latter meaning is more probable and I have given instructions that free issues be given to all personnel of this health-giving and invigorating spirit.

(f). My Batman was at one time apprenticed to a racing stable owned by Atty Persse. He is confident that this exercise refers to polo. He has himself ridden a winner on the flat and speaks with some authority, and he assures me that no self-respecting jockey would participate.

Table 5. Exercise

(c). My next trick is impossible.

(d). Contemplation of this old-world exercise brings a reassurance of faith and the certain knowledge that all is right with the world.

(g). I see no point in this exercise, as we all know how difficult it is to balance when you're whistled.

2. It is impossible that the above comments may be of use to your OTU, and it would be greatly appreciated if you inform this unit of any difficulties you yourselves may have experienced.

Group Captain, Commanding,
Royal Air Force Station,
CHARTER HALL

Lorenz Visual System

The following extract has been reproduced with kind permission from GeoCities:

The Lorenz system had been in use in military and civil aircraft in several countries since the mid-1930s to enable pilots to land at airfields at night and in bad weather. It was essentially a system whereby two direction-beam aerials were placed so that they radiated two wide beams of a radio signal which overlapped along the centre line of the airfield runway. The aerials were automatically alternately switched to the transmitter so that one radiated only Morse dots and the other dashes. The spacing of the dots and dashes was such that where the beams overlapped, the dots and dashes joined to give a continuous note, known as the equi-signal, was very narrow indeed and quite accurate enough for a pilot with a suitable receiver to land on the exact centre line of the runway. The frequencies used internationally for this purpose were between 28 and 35mHz. The Lorenz technique was simple, but it called for a high standard of flying on the part of the pilot, who had to be very proficient in the difficult art of instrument-flying, that is flying without reference to a visual horizon. Initially, while about fifteen to twenty miles away, the aircraft Lorenz receiver would be tuned to the appropriate frequency; then the pilot, if his aircraft was to the left of the airfield runway, would hear morse dots in his earphones; he would then steer his aircraft to the right until the dots became a steady note: the equi-signal. At that point he would have to turn left; if he did not turn far enough, the steady note would turn into dashes; too much, and he would be flying into the dot zone again. Thus, by making small alterations left or right of his course, as indicated by the dots or dashes, he would be able to keep in the equi-signal

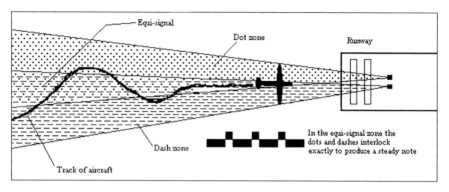

Pictorial view of the Lorenz Visual System. (Courtesy of GeoCities)

and thus be aligned with the unseen runway. As he got nearer, the beam got narrower and more accurate until, at touchdown, it was less than the width of the runway. The accuracy of the system was such that a skilled beam pilot could detect a shift of a hundredth of the equi-signal width.

Report on G.A.F Night Fighting from the Interrogation of Prisoners

An official Air Ministry report was compiled at the end of the Second World War detailing the Luftwaffe's night fighter viewpoint of flying and fighting at night, documenting their successes and failures in aerial combat. A copy of this report was kept in Bertie's personal belongings.

We spent ten days interrogating various types of Hun starting at the Air Ministry level where we found that little information was available, working up through Groups to the aircrew themselves on the evidence of whom most of the following report is based.

The first day started in a rather John Buchan way with Mercedes and Hun chauffeurs rolling up to the door. Luckier than most British women drivers were heavily scented and they drove us out to a nearby pine forest where 'LUFTFLOTTEREICH' (Fighter Command approx.) were living in caravans having fled from Berlin before Russian advance.

Here we were met by a tall Hun Officer looking like any old Austrian Count out of any rather second rate musical comedy. He ushered us into a large marquee where we sat down on one side of a table with the Hun

Staff officer on the other. The Chief of Staff was a typical film Hun called Oberstleutnant Kessel with a pink and white pomaded face and coarse hands with shaped and polished nails. He commanded one of the famous bomber squadrons in the Blitz days and was still clanking with the decorations of a grateful Germany. Apart from him, his staff consisted of a motley crew more conspicuous for their suave staff work than for their Nordic ancestry.

It was in this atmosphere that we began to learn the official view. As we left the interrogation the Huns saluted and clicked their heels. Thorough the window of the car I saw Kessel walking up and down, his gloved hands crooked behind his back tapping knuckle to palm like Conrad Veidt in almost any British film of the 1920s. Our next visit took us to a Jagl Division (Group) where we interrogated two AOCs, and their staffs. Here the type of Hun was similar, and again one was conscious of a plethora of Ritterkreus, Iron Crosses, and golden wings, jack boots and elegant breeches flanked with scarlet stripes.

Karl Kessel (1 June 1912 – 24 August 1997) held the rank of Oberstleutnant and Geschwaderkommodore of Kampfgeschwader 2 in 1940. He became general in the armed forces of West Germany. He was a recipient of the Knight's Cross of the Iron Cross, awarded on the 23 January 1944. Kessel joined the Bundeswehr in 1956 and retired in 1970 as a Generalmajor. (Courtesy of SJS)

It was not however till we reached the aircrew themselves that we met people who seemed to know their job. The first station we visited was EGGEBECK which was miles from anywhere, a sort of Great Massingham. Here they told us a little rhyme which had a certain recognisable aircrew flavour about it; 'Vorner Dreck hinton Dreck in der Mitte Eggebeck'. Even here the type of man was somewhat difficult from his English counterpart. In enthusiasm and skill they were outstanding, but their flashy arrogant attitude was unattractive and very unfamiliar. Major Schnaufer the ace top scorer, with 121 four-engined bombers destroyed to his credit, was a thin tall dago-looking pilot of about 27 with swarthy complexion and rather long hair. He wore a high Hun peaked cap suitably thumbed and twisted in true aircrew style and a mass of medals including the Ritterkreus with oak leaves, swords and diamonds, a magnificent affair that any dowager would be proud to wear on her corsage. There were other types of course, including scruffy Huns and lazy Huns, clean Huns, and dreary Huns and on the whole a comparable Hun for most of the well-known British types.

Major Heinz-Wolfgang Schnaufer German Luftwaffe night-fighter pilot and the highest-scoring night fighter ace in the history of aerial warfare. A flying ace is a military aviator credited with shooting down five or more enemy aircraft during combat. All Schnaufer's 121 victories were claimed during World War II, mostly against British four-engine bombers, for which he was awarded the Knight's Cross of the Iron Cross with Oak Leaves, Swords and Diamonds, Germany's highest military decoration at the time, on 16 October 1944. He was nicknamed 'The Spook of St Trond', from the location of his unit's base in occupied Belgium. (Courtesy of 12 OCH)

PART II

General Report

Although Senior Staff Officers at 'Luftlotte Reich' stated that the low and high level 'Intruders' had caused little embarrassment to the G.A.F. it became plain when talking to the Staff of the 'Jagd Division' that this was not so and considerable disorganisation and loss of efficiency had resulted. On interrogating the actual crews this became even more significant and it is now quite obvious that the Mosquito long range fighter by undermining morale of the Huns crews played an important part in limiting their success against the bombers. The views of the higher formation should therefore be discounted and the report taken from the detailed evidence of the crews.

A fairly representative cross section of about 20 night fighter crews have been questioned closely including single engine pilots, jet pilots, but more especially Ju.88 and Me.110 pilots and observers. These include two ace pilots, one test pilot and one operational research navigator radio. In all a total of 29 hours was spent in actual interrogation.

Hun crews were under the impression that British Night Fighters were available to attack them at take-off, on the way to the beacons, on the way to the bomber stream which they thought was flanked with Mosquitos, in the target area, on the way home and their airfields when attempting to land.

They thought that all their transmissions were homed on and so against orders from superior formations would, whenever possible, switch off all apparatus which transmitted. This meant that their IFF (Fu.25A) provided less protection to them and sometimes resulted in disaster. Oberleutnant Welter states that a friend of his was shot down three times recently over Berlin by Hun flak, possibly for this reason. It also meant that they were faced with the alternative of flying low without radio altimeters and therefore 'pranging' or switching them on and being homed on by our fighters.

As a result, then of the advent of the Mosquito in force last Autumn they were made to change their tactics and this seriously reduced their efficiency. That they must change was considered vital, not only psychologically, but also from the material losses alone. One Geschwade with a strength of about 100 crews lost in 3 months, from mid-November 1944, 24 crews dead, 10 missing and 15 wounded.

It was then in the autumn of last year that the real 'Mosquito panik' started and from then on all the normal run of crashes through natural causes were attributed to the Mosquito. This increased its reputation and their despondency.

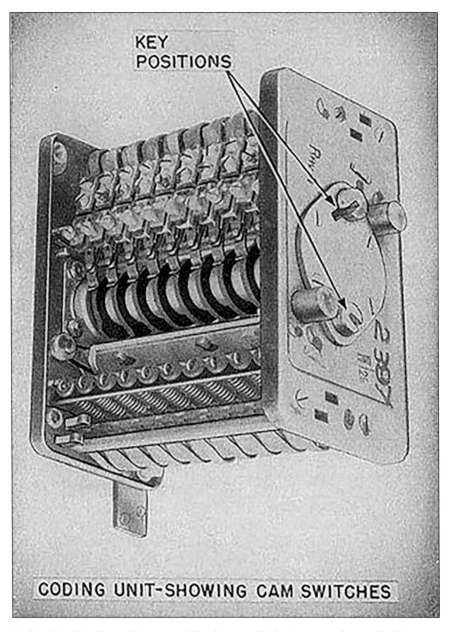

KEY
POSITIONS

CODING UNIT-SHOWING CAM SWITCHES

FuG 25a Erstling (German: 'Firstborn', 'Debut', sometimes FuGe) was an identification friend or foe (IFF) transponder installed in Luftwaffe aircraft starting in 1941 in order to allow German Freya radar stations to identify them as friendly. The system was also used as a navigation transponder as part of the EGON night bombing system during 1943 and 1944. It was the second IFF system to be used, replacing the FuG 25 Zwilling. (Courtesy of 12 OCH)

Oberleutnant Kurt Welter (25 February 1916 – 7 March 1949), pictured right, was a German Luftwaffe fighter ace and the most successful jet expert of the Second World War. A flying ace or fighter ace is a military aviator credited with shooting down five or more enemy aircraft during aerial combat. He claimed a total of 63 aerial victories that is, 63 aerial combat encounters resulting in the destruction of the enemy aircraft achieved in 93 combat missions. He recorded 56 victories at night, including 33 Mosquitos, and scored more aerial victories from a jet fighter aircraft than anyone else in World War II and possibly in aviation history. However this score is a matter of controversy; research of Royal Air Force losses suggests Welter overclaimed Mosquito victories considerably. Against this, Luftwaffe claims were very strict, requiring confirmation and proof by witnesses. The remains of aircraft shot down and crashed would be verifiable and recorded on the ground in the sector claimed. (Courtesy of 12 OCH)

Major Schnaufer, the top scoring ace, was voluble on the subject. He attributed his survival to the fact that he did not only weave but actually carried out what he described as 'steep turns' from take-off to landing. He even continued to weave when in AI contact with a bomber and he told of one night when he was about to open fire on a Lancaster when his look-out gunner reported a Mosquito about to open fire on him. He immediately peeled off. Lost the Lancaster but did finally shake off the Mosquito. The only time they felt at all free from our fighters was in the stream but as he said, 'the above story and others made it impossible to relax even then'. His impression was that none but the Hun aces dared to climb till the last moment and all remained very low near the beacons which they knew that we manned. It was called flying at 'Ritterkreus Level', as if you flew higher you would never survive to receive your decoration. Captain Krasue, with 29 destroyed, quoted an instance in the Ruhr when he was intercepted in the target area and pursued for 45 minutes having frequent visuals on a Mosquito as it came into range. He took violent evasive action in azimuth and height and by going through cloud but this failed

Kapitan Johannes Krause, preferred to be known as Hans, awarded the German Cross in Gold on 10 September 1944, serving as a Oberleutnant with 6./NJ 101, and Knights Cross on 7 February 1945, when commanding II./NG 101. He ended the war with 28 night victories. (Courtesy Traces at War)

to shake off the fighter. He finally succeeded in evading only by flying to a district in the Ardennes that he knew really well, flying as he said, 'down a valley below the level of the hills'. This confirmed in his mind, the exceptional standard of AI. His Navigator-Radio reported that one night he remembered having had six rear contacts on believed Mosquitos. Three of these he saw. He also confirmed that evasive action was carried out all the time, even when a tail warner was being used and even when in contact with a bomber.

It seems they had far less confidence in their tail gunners warners than we did and it became the custom in the Bf110 for the second man to act as Navigator and W.T. Operator, and the third man to have the sole job of searching visually for Mosquitos and firing the gun if he should get a chance. One Navigator Radio said, 'After all the eye is really the best form of Radar'.

All crews said that after the 'Mosquito panik' they flew at treetop to the beacons. Fifty metres was quoted even on dark nights and 30 metres when waiting permission to land. An alternative technique of returning to base provided you could come straight in and land was to approach straight from 1,000 feet.

This Captain Krauser preferred to do when possible for as he said, 'it had the added advantage that if you were shot down by a Mosquito you had plenty of time to bale out'.

Their demoralisation was demonstrated still further when a pilot referred to 'the late autumn when the German defensive fighters had themselves been forced onto the defensive' and had even to resort to throwing out 'window' as a routine, to mislead and distract the Mosquito fighters.

As an example of their sorry plight they spoke about the night 4–5 December 1944 when the Mosquito menace reached its peak and registered itself strongly on their minds. On this night there was a spoof on DORTMUND while the Main Force attacked HEILBRONN and KARSRUHE. The Hun night fighters were all sent to the spoof and waited there for about 15 minutes for the attack to start. However, they found nothing but high intruders and their losses were very serious indeed. On that night 100 Group fighters destroyed six and probably a seventh. So far it has been impossible to establish what the claims of H.Q.F.C. and 85 Group were.

It is also of interest that they did not seen to be very much afraid of the guns from a four-engined bomber provided they made an attack as opposed to a stalking approach. They reckoned they could usually fire before being noticed and that this applied even to AGLT, of which they had a fairly accurate polar diagram, whose limitations they thought they could exploit. The tactic was not necessarily to use upward firing guns which were only used by probably 40–50 per cent of crews who had such guns fitted.

Another point was reported that by the time the Mosquito came into operation the Bf110 had had its day, except for really good crews, as it was too slow and manoeuvrable. The Ju.88 was also considered to be outclassed by the Mosquito both in climbing and level speed. On the other hand, if it came to the point of having to evade it was simpler in a Ju.88 and they knew the Mosquito found it difficult to climb efficiently at slow speeds. A slow climbing turn full throttle was an accepted method of evading.

In general, it appeared that the fear of the Mosquito was the last straw which made their difficult life almost hopeless, except for a few night fighter aces. Their communications were jammed. One crew said that of about 20 frequencies available 19 would almost certainly be jammed and any but a good crew would probably have no communications with the ground even on WT. Their AI was jammed by electrical jammers and rendered useless and as often as not if they did get orders they would probably lead them to the spoof target.

On the night of 21 February when Schnaufer claims 7 destroyed he was ordered to the spoof target by ground control but he thought he knew better, as in fact he did, and went against orders to the real target.

Into all this came the Mosquito. Fear of homing combined with a healthy respect for our centimetre AI forced a change of tactics. Lights were reduced to a minimum for take-off and landing. All flights to and around the beacon were at ground level. This increased flying accidents and lead to a disobedience to ground orders which often placed them poorly for reaching the stream in time. One crew said that many never went to the beacons, after all we were not a 'suicide club'. He used the English phrase. Again, they stressed that as a result of remaining low they arrived late when the bombers had already bombed and were on their way home.

As a final comment it is only fair to say that as a result of the avalanche of difficulties under which they worked they had a ridiculously exaggerated idea of their vulnerability from the long range fighters.

PART III
DETAILED ANSWERS TO QUESTIONS

Why was There Recently a Fall in the Number of British Claims

1. The numbers were severely reduced owing to the lack of petrol. In March they were ordered to reduce their already diminished sorties by three times.
2. The so called 'young hares' (P/Os Prune) were not allowed to fly at all but only the established aces who knew all the answers.
3. Tail warner's and boozers were fitted.
4. An extra body was carried whose express and only job was to watch out visually for Mosquitos.
5. All pilots carried out violent weaving from take-off to landing.
6. They had begun to fit type F flashing IR lamps in the tails of their aircraft.
7. They carried ten centimetre 'Window' which they threw out wherever they felt in danger which was most of the time.

Why didn't They Intrude Over England

Nearly all the crews we met were very keen to intrude over England and were fully conscious of the chaos they could have caused and the success they could have achieved even without AI, which was good at low heights. They had repeatedly attempted to sell the idea since early in the War, but it seems that it was forbidden at the highest possible level by Hitler and Goering.

Whatever the original reason it became almost impossible recently owing to petrol shortage. In spite of this, the ace Major Schnaufer had a meeting with Goering last autumn and received permission for a certain amount of petrol to be released for an operation, the code word for which was GIESELE. This was no more than intruding on the heavies when they were landing in England. The operation was to take place at the end of November and they expected to shoot down about 80 bombers the first night.

Just before it took place however they heard that we knew about it and it was postponed until we should have relaxed our vigilance.

This was the background to the night of 3 March. On this night the Hun service heard the Master Bomber telling the heavies to hurry up with their bombing. This was interpreted as fore knowledge by us of their operation, as a result of which we were said to have been fully prepared and they therefore had arrived late. Their losses were 20 and not significantly less than their claims. It was therefore considered a failure and except for a few further sorties by individual crews the whole thing was dropped, this time finally.

How wrong were we!

There was another operation which Schnaufer had suggested but as he said, 'it was so slow getting permission through the official channels, that the war was over before it was granted.' He was ready to put it into operation early in January. It was called FEUERSEE. He intended to use his whole GESCHWADE (N.J.G.4) comprising about 60 aircraft. They were to fly out across the North Sea at sea level using radio altimeters, towards a WT beacon which they say they often used near Orfordness. If this was not on they would turn on DR. When about 15 miles from England they would set course for Ostend which they said was Bomber Command's routine way home. At that height they would get almost no sea returns and therefore an excellent maximum range on their SN2. When in contact with the bombers which might even have lights on they were to climb and destroy. He realised this would probably only work once but on that one occasion he hoped to destroy about 100 aircraft. How right he was!

Flying Control

By the time it was likely crews would have to take-off they would already be sitting in their aircraft. Originally they received instructions to take off by stars or rockets from the control tower but they had learnt that this attracted intruder and so latterly they would have a green light flashed at them.

For assisting in landing flying control was often fitted with a Naxes which would give a bearing on an AI equipped intruder and this was checked by plots from the No.1 Radar site (Sector). The FCO would then give a pilot permission to land, who would then come from wherever he was waiting. Each crew had his own pet place about 8 miles away from the airfield. When he was approaching the VL he would again ask permission and this would only be granted if the Intruder was badly placed for an interception.

Bombing with small bombs by Intruders only prevented take off if they were on the runway. Immediately after an attack, a car with a searchlight would drive down the runway and provided there was no bomb actually on it, permission to take off would be given at once. Driving the car was not popular as it had been shot up on several occasions.

They were conscious that firing of ESNs gave their position away to us and the old hands at the game did this as little as possible. They did not necessarily do left hand circuits or indeed circuits at all. If they had to do a circuit it was just as often right hand.

In moonlight they very often took off and landed without any lights at all. If they used any for take-off it was often only one glim lamp halfway down the runway and a vertical searchlight a mile off the end of the runway. For landing they would come in on VHF.B.A. and only ask for lights if they had to, which would then be cowled and only visible downwind from a height of about 150 feet.

Enemy airfields became less used recently but large numbers of real airfields were used. They set great store dispersal and after their NFT they would disperse their aircraft on many local airfields, so that if lighting was necessary they could let the airfield furthest from the intruder light up and then as this attracted the Mosquito they would let fighters off from the field he had just abandoned.

Originally they had signs in the form of red flashing lights and pyrotechnics to show these were intruders but recently it was assumed there would always be an intruder for landing. One pilot told us that the FCO. would ring up dispersal and say: 'the duty instructor has arrived'. We were surprised to find that they did normally get back to their home airfield and elaborate diversions were not perhaps so usual as had been thought.

Squadron Routine

They never had a day or night off, officially at any rate and it seems their tour could only be ended by illness or death. The Station and its Commander were no more than the hotel and its proprietor with no operational control.

The groundcrew consisted of an establishment of about 500 per GRUPPE (Squadron) of which they in fact had about 300 including WAAF. The Station also had a small repair party for engine changes etc, which remained when the Squadron moved. The general feeling seemed to be that greater efficiency would have been achieved by all servicing and maintenance being done by a permanent Station staff who would work for whatever Squadron was stationed there.

They were distracted with the Intelligence system. Their interrogation was hardly over anything more than filling in a form and there was no responsible specialist officer to ferret out information for them. This they had to do themselves as best they could. They knew of our system and thought it was much better.

At dusk they would have a Met briefing where apart from the actual weather, the official view would be given of the likelihood of bombing by the enemy. The probability was embodied in the general state of readiness 'Dove' or 'Eagle'. If 'Eagle' then they would mostly be at 15 minutes and some actually in their cockpit. If 'Dove' then they would be at 30 minutes in dispersal. Their dispersal huts were made more luxurious than ours. They had a dining room, sitting room and bedrooms. After the night they would sleep till luncheon. They would then check that the DIs were complete and all snags had been cleared. A short 20 minute NFT would then follow and they would park their aircraft ready for its night take off, quite possibly

A camouflaged Luftwaffe hangar at Audembert airfield, designated 372, Northern France, housing single Me 109E, believed to be from JG 26. (Courtesy of Alantikwall.com)

at some other airfield on the principle of dispersal. They were amazed to hear that we left our aircraft out on the airfield. They all had small, heated hangars; they considered this a *sine qua non* for night flying aircraft.

PFF Over Berlin

Many attempts had been made during the war to deal with PFF Mosquito attacks on Berlin but it was only towards the end that they had met with any real success. Oberleutnant Welter was last summer a test pilot at Rechlin. He was commissioned to find a solution to the problem. They had tried the Me 109 and the Fw 190 but neither could really catch the Mosquitos, and even fitting the *'water injection'* and what they called *'ice injection'* system to the Me 109, although these increased the speed they also damaged the engines. The jet was considered the answer and he was to say whether the Arado 234 or Me 262 would be the more suitable.

He flew both and operated last September, actually destroying a Mosquito with an Me 262 during that month in searchlights, over Berlin. At the same time he asked that a two seater with AI be constructed. This only went into operation at the end of the war. It was however his opinion that herein lay the final solution, and plans were in hand to bring many more into operation. They had tried this model of AI earlier in Fw 190 and Me.109 but

The Arado Ar 234, this *'wonder aircraft'*, was first test flown on 15 June 1943, entering operational service in September 1944 with a number of this type going to KG 76. A total of 274 were produced, with only 100 estimated to see combat. It was brought into service too late to change the tide of the war for the Third Reich (Author's Collection)

it had been unsatisfactory. The unsuitability of the aircraft made it valueless to continue trials.

In the meantime with a few single seater Me.262, great success had been achieved, at any rate according to their claims. Although a start was made in September and a few sorties were carried out in the following months, it was only in January that more than single aircraft operated. Up to the end of the war they had carried out 70 night sorties altogether and had shot down 48 Mosquitos for the loss of only one due to ramming. They operated under close ground control similar to our GCI and the searchlights helped them in the last stage. The searchlights were manned by women and the slogan was *'once the girls have got you, you've had it'*.

From about January they operated at a Flight from Burg and later when this was bombed, from an autobahn. The critical point was their endurance which was at the most 1¼ hours and normally not more than 55 minutes. They were helped they said by the routine routing and timing of the PFF attacks which they grew to know. The raids were referred to as the London-Berlin Express and the three normal Northern Central and Southern routes called Platforms 1, 2, and 3 respectively. They were almost the only fighters still capable of using close ground control as unless there was a simultaneous Main Force raid, their communications and AI were unaffected by jamming. They were too fast to intercept four-engined bombers with ease as unless skilfully piloted the flame in the jet would go out. Welter himself had however shot down two Lancasters.

While they were operating with Me 262 over Berlin their success had already been accepted as sufficient to satisfy the silencing of the flak while they were operating. The advent of AI, which would last they said until PFF flew jamming aircraft with their units, would enable them to operate in bad weather which up to date had paid poor dividends. Welter remembered and asked about the night when we sent Mosquito fighters in a wave in front of the bombers. He alone flew on that occasion ands claimed a damaged (F/Lt. Leyland, No 157 Squadron)*. He criticised our timing however, and said he had time to land at Burg, refuel and be up again for PFF, one of

---

* *Flight Lieutenant J.H. Leyland flew on the night of 2–3 April 1945 carrying out a spoof raid on Berlin, with 8 other squadron Mosquitos, supporting 8 Group operations. Having be identified by searchlights Leutnant Welter in his Me.262 saw his chance to attack, making four individual attacks, with two strikes being recorded. Leyland managed to escape his attacker after spinning his aircraft and heading for home*

which he destroyed. There were plans for fitting BERLIN or BREMEN centimetre AI in the Me.262 and also upward firing guns.

Radar

The aircrews were AI conscious, particularly the experienced ones, but the combination of inferior equipment and radio countermeasures forced them to rely more on visual aids as the war progressed. When LICHTENSTEIN, their first AI, was being effectively jammed and also homed upon, a new mark was brought into operation, in the late months of 1943 called SN2. This apparatus is very similar to our Mark IV, both in performance and presentation, except that the earlier models had only one tube with a changeover switch for azimuth and elevation. At first minimum range was so poor that both LICHTENSTEIN and SN2 were fitted into some machines, making this aerial array more like an airman's bedstead than ever. The rearward coverage of 3,000ft was increased by the installation tail aerial, and by use of a two way switch, the Navigator could look either forwards or backwards.

Later modifications included two tubes instead of one. Many operators preferred to keep single tube presentation. Trials were carried out on a new aerial array, as the original forest of aerials cut down the aircraft speed by 20 kilometres per hour and was very disconcerting for the pilot particularly when polarised at an angle of 45 degrees, which was done in a vain attempt to overcome the jamming. Electrical jamming against SN2 was started in July 1944 and from that time its effectiveness as an AI deteriorated rapidly. The extensive use of Window was another nail in the coffin, although, as usual the best crews found ways of working through it. In fact some claimed that the presence of Window on the tube indicated the proximity of the bomber stream and was in some degree therefore an aid. Later modification known as TANUS was fitted, similar to that used by Freya Ground Stations, to enable the Navigator to differentiate between Aircraft Echoes and Window.

Homing on the SN2 jammers was possible by highly skilled crews, but as the frequency was in harmony with their own ground Gee jammers, they often homed on these. German industry was producing SN2 in such large quantities that in spite of its ineffectiveness, squadrons were still being equipped with it. In an attempt to overcome the jamming, a modification

A RAF Lancaster of 101 Squadron, dropping Window on a bombing raid over Duisburg, 1944, to confuse the Third Reich's radars (Courtesy of T. Church)

was introduced, by which the frequency of the equipment could be changed in the air. This was known as SN3 and was still at the experimental stage. The development and use of NAXOS, (a homer on to H.S.2) was being carried on at the same time. NAXOS was first used to home on the bombers in August 1943 when the main force attacked Hanover, and from then on proved a great success until the use of H.2.S. was restricted. A technique was evolved whereby the fighter started low down and climbed up in steps and could so home on to individual aircraft without having to use SN2. Because of production difficulties, only about 20 per cent of the total force had NAXOS.

FLENSBURG was used extensively against Monica but was discarded when Bomber Command took Monica out of their aircraft. FUGE 216 and

217 (NEPTUNE) proved to be rather an unreliable tail warner, although one Navigator claimed it was his 'life insurance'. Twin seater Me 262 and Fw 190 and Me 109 and a certain number of Me 110s were equipped with FUGE 218, a forward looking version of FUGE 217, which could be fitted with a Pilot's indicator and had not yet been electronically jammed. The presentation was similar to SN2, maximum range ¾ kilometres, minimum range 200/300 metres. In spite of protests from the pilots, many navigators did not use visors. Instead red filters were fitted over the tubes to prevent flashing lights in the cockpit. The crews were quite convinced, rightly so in the last two months of the war, that we were homing on to their IFF, so contrary to orders they seldom switched it on, thus undermining the whole air to ground recognition system.

The AOC of JD2 was asked what it was that our Perfectos fitted aircraft homed on the ground near STADE. He and his staff burst out laughing. It seems that although the official view was that it was impossible for us to home on their IFF a civilian scientist living to the west of Hamburg disbelieved this. He set up an IFF on his roof and hoped to catch a Mosquito homing onto it. His experiment was an unqualified success. The same fear existed over their radio altimeters, with the result that several crews flew into the ground because of turning it off. In early 1945 one GRUPPE of NJG 4 were equipped with BERLIN-GERAET, a ten centimetre AI. It was not until the first H.2.S. set was captured that the German scientists turned their attention to centimetre equipment. This AI was first used in February 1945 with very poor results, which was hardly surprising since the maximum range was about 3 kilometres and minimum range of 1 kilometre. It needed a lot of servicing and had endless teething troubles. The presentation was similar to Mk.1V and the scanner direction mechanically operated, and orders given accordingly to the position of the lever: There was a further development in the trial stage called BREMEN GERAET. This was similar in every way to BERLIN and so suitable for smaller aircraft.

A far more sinister development early in 1945 was that known as KIEL GERAET, an infra-red homer on the bombers' exhausts. The maximum range when approaching from below was 5/6 kilometres. The presentation was similar to Mark VIII but being a homer it gave no range. However an experienced operator could obtain an approximate range from the look of the picture, and at minimum range four pictures, one from each exhaust, were visible. The moon was an embarrassment and it was useless near the target because of the fires – one night the fires of Dortmund were homed on from Kassel. The device would work through thin haze but not through cloud.

A Boozer against centimetre equipment called NAXOS HALBE was still very much in the experimental stage. Several new marks of FLENSBURG were being worked on, with the intention of homing upon most of our jamming aircraft. German aircrew had a good knowledge of our radar aids, talking of Magic Box, Fishpond, Village Inn, Grille (Mark XV) and Frankfurt Geraet (Mark X). NJG 1, had already fitted Type F lamps in the tails of their aircraft with a flashing light which they thought would probably be sufficient. NJG 4 were on the point of fitting not only this but also Type Z in the nose.

Air to Ground Communications

Allied jamming almost nullified the enemy's ground to air communication system. They were forced to give up VHF and use HF and when that was jammed morse was introduced. This, in its turn was jammed, but good Wireless Operators were usually able to read messages through interference. An apparatus known as BERNADINE was being developed which printed the message on a tape in front of the pilot. This was not yet in use on operations. The Hun navigation and commentary beacons were interfered with by us by a system known as MEACONING. This picked up the transmission and relayed it from a point in England, so that the D/F loop would give a fix somewhere between the two transmitters making it useless as a navigation aid.

The communications between aircraft and local flying control were not seriously affected. When asked whether they used their wireless sets to home onto our aircraft they were furious to find they had never thought of it.

Miscellaneous Points of Interest

1. The Ju.188 was not used as a fighter but flew in small numbers during bomber raids listening to the frequencies on which our navigational aids were operating so that they could subsequently jam them.
2. It seems there has been little training over the last 6 months and they were living on their fat. Previously it had taken place chiefly in the Munich area, at a time when it was rather beyond the range of our intruders.

3. They were surprised by the accuracy of the 1943 intruders on French airfields before the days of GEE. They thought we must have been helped by the French. They remembered a night at St.Trond when they had been to the cinema. The weather was shocking and the only way they found their way back to the airfield was to drive in the general direction of the noise of the British intruder's engines.

4. Air to Air identification had not been solved by them but they did not consider it a problem as the four-engined bombers were what they were after and nobody could mistake them. They did not use resin lights and there is no explanation of the light seen by many pilots, inboard of the starboard engine on the Me 110.

5. They reckoned that 9/10 of their successes were scored by a few ace crews.

6. There is no explanation for the phenomenon described as a He 219 with rocket assisted climb. The He 219 itself was in short supply. It had originally been considered for use against the Mosquito but it was abandoned in view of the success of the Me 262.

7. The Me 410 was not used at all as a night fighter.

8. The crews themselves seemed to know a great deal about '*DIE HUNDERSTE GRUPPE*' including the name of the AOC and some of the stations. One crew when they heard we were intruders said. 'Are you perhaps from Little Snoring?'

9. Medals were doled out on the basis of points. You received 1 point for a single engined aircraft, 3 for a four-engined by day, 4 for a four-engined by night and 5 for a Mosquito. That is to say that Schnaufer with 121 kills has probably about 480 points.

10. One crew to whom we spoke had been stationed on the Russian front. In his words 'night fighting was so difficult there because the Russians were so backward in radar that they had no transmissions onto which we could home'. It seems that the Russians never did anything but sporadic bombing. This could have been dealt with by our GCI and unjammed AI but it would have been too great an undertaking to cover the whole front and the comparatively little damage they caused did not justify the expense or effort.

11. In view of the chaos caused by jamming of radar and signals generally they were on the point of starting a new tactic – depending upon visual aids only. Every observer corps post was to have a small

searchlight and rockets. In good weather the bomber stream would be marked by every post switching on its light when the bombers were overhead and then dipping it in the direction in which the bombers were flying. In bad weather the same service would be provided by rockets. They were waiting for all posts to be supplied before starting and they thought they would have been ready about the end of May.

12. When asked why they used tracer they denied that they did so and asked us why we used green tracer. This we denied.

13. It seems quite certain that far from attempting to engage our Mosquitos they avoided them like the plague. They knew of no case when a Hun night fighter had destroyed an intruder but this does not of course mean that none were in fact shot down. There was however no organised counter offensive to our counter offensive.

14. Although GCI procedures had long been abandoned for the running commentary method of control, it was still available if we changed our tactics from concentration to dilution.

15. CORNA never fooled them. They recognised the voices as unfamiliar. They also said they thought it was most unimaginatively done by us.

16. On being told how we used to use their visual navigational aids, they told us that they would often have been lost had it for not been for the searchlights of the Brussels diver gun belt.

17. They had the same idea as us about reducing the graticule in the gunsight and preferred red to any other colour.

18. Night glasses were used by some people but against big bombers they were not really necessary.

19. They never had AI beacons.

20. They were jealous of our system of operational trials and most critical of theirs. When a piece of equipment was demanded it was produced by Siemens or Telefunken and sent to WannEuchen where it was test flown by non-operational deadbeats, who always held up the trials and gave the wrong answer. A unit such as the FIU did not exist.

21. All the secrets of their newest equipment had been given to the Japanese before the capitulation.

Epilogue

All the crews we saw talked of the Mosquito with bated breath. 'If only we had Mosquitos with your AI,' said one squadron commander. Another time we were told that the night fighters' prayer was:

'DEAREST HERMANN GIVE ME A MOSQUITO'

ABBREVIATIONS

AASF	Advanced Air Striking Force
AC	Air Command
ACFE	Air Command, Far East
ACSEA	Air Command, South East Asia
ADGB	Air Defence Great Britain
AFC	Air Force Cross
AHQ	Air Headquarters
AI	Airborne Interception
AOC	Air Officer Commanding
AORNWA	Air Operations Room North-Western Area
API	Armoured Piercing Incendiary
ASH	Air to Surface H
AVM	Air Vice Marshal
BAOR	British Army of the Rhine
BF	Baverische Flugzeugwerke
CO	Commanding Officer
DFC	Distinguished Flying Cross
DFM	Distinguished Flying Medal
DSC	Distinguished Service Cross

ABBREVIATIONS

DSO	Distinguished Service Order
E/A	Enemy Aircraft
ERFTS	Elementary and Reserve Flying Training School
ENSA	Entertainment National Service Association
ETA	Estimated Time of Arrival
FCO	Fighter Controller Officer
FIS	Flying Instructors School
F/L	Flight Lieutenant
FT	Feet
FTS	Flying Training School
GAF	German Air Force
G/Cpt	Group Captain
GOC	General Officer Commanding
HE	High Explosive
He	Heinkel
HM	His Majesty
HR	Hours
IFF	Identification, Friend or Foe
IR	Infra Red
JG	Jagdgeschwader
Ju	Junkers
Knt	Knots
KG	Kampgeschwader
LAC	Leading Aircraftsman
MC	Military Cross
ME	Messerschmitt

Mph	Miles per hour
MiD	Mention in Dispatches
MK	Mark
MO	Medical Officer
MT	Motor Transport
NCO	Non-Commissioned Officer
NJG	Nachtjagdgeschwader
OR	Ordinary Ranks
ORB	Operational Record Book
OTU	Operational Training Unit
PFF	Pathfinder Force
PMC	President of Mess Committee
P/O	Pilot Officer
PT	Physical Training
PTSD	Post Traumatic Stress Disorder
RAF	Royal Air Force
RAAF	Royal Australian Air Force
RCAF	Royal Canadian Air Force
RFC	Royal Flying Corps
RNZAF	Royal New Zealand Air Force
R/T	Radio Telegraphy
SEAC	South East Asia Command
SHAEF	Supreme Headquarters Allied Expeditionary Force
SQN	Squadron
USAAF	United States Army Air Force
VHF	Very High Frequency

ABBREVIATIONS

VIP	Very Important Person
VL	Visual Lorenz
WAAF	Women's Auxiliary Air Force
W/T	Wireless Telegraphy

INDEX

112 ASR, 165

114 ASR, 162

1419 Special duties Flight, 128

2 Squadron, 65

23 Squadron, 30–1, 46, 56, 63, 99, 112, 114, 116, 122–3, 125, 128, 130, 134–6, 140, 170, 180, 186

84 Squadron, 155

115 Squadron, 111

157 Squadron, 218

169 Squadron, 112

171 Squadron, 179

207 Squadron, 13–14

418 Squadron, 46

515 Squadron, 112, 114–15, 117, 127, 140

605 Squadron, 75–81, 90, 101, 103

No.7 FIS, 119

29 M.U., 68

34 M.U., 67

51 OTU, 65

60 OTU, 65

132 OTU, 65

3 Group, 111

5 Group, 119

9 Group, 86

10 Group, 47

11 Group, 43, 81

81 Group, 65

100 Group, 111, 117, 125, 183

HQ, ACSEA, 148

1./KG 6, 90

I./JG 300, 100

5./NJG, 78

IV./KG 1, 34

III./KG 40, 42

IV./KG 40, 57

III./KG 53, 31

Abbeville [airfield], 30

Addison, AVM Edward, 183

Air Defence Great Britain, 13

Aitken, W/C Russell, 81, 89, 98

Aldergrove, RAF [airfield], 15

Aldworth, Richard, 92

Amberley, RAAF [airfield], 167

Amiens [airfield], 47, 52

Anson [aircraft], 14, 167

ASH [Radar], 125, 127, 135

Audaxes [aircraft], 8

Avord [airfield], 55–6

Ayr, RAF [airfield], 112

INDEX

Badly, Douglas, 122, 180–5
Baker, Charles, 155
Barton Hall, RAF [airfield], 86
Bather, GO, 137
Batzoff, Douglas, 160
BBC, 87, 152
Bearsted, AC Lord, 105
Beaudet, Paul, 182
Beauvais [airfield], 42, 98
Becke, Raymond, 162, 164–5
Beecroft, GO, 137
Bergen, 82
Berlin, 100, 207
Bf110 [aircraft], 78, 207, 212
Bircham Newton, RAF [airfield], 13
Bleak House, 2,
Blenheim [aircraft], 29–32, 65
Boller, Paul, 57
Bond, Geoffery, 115
Boston [aircraft], 29, 47, 49, 52, 54
Brackley, AC Herbert, 160
Bracknell, RAF, 148
Bradwell Bay, RAF [airfield], 46,
    75, 81, 89, 98, 103
Brussels, 81, 95
Bullmore, Herbert, 173
Burg, 100, 218

Caen, 39, 47, 52, 123
Cambrai [airfield], 114
Castle Camps, RAF [airfield], 75,
    79–81
Catalina [aircraft], 162, 165
Chartres [airfield], 55
Chievres, 90
Clark, John, 157
Cloncurry, RAAF [airfield], 161–2

Collins, Henry, 78
Colvin, Walter, 155, 167
Condor [aircraft], 57
Conquer, Norman, 65
Copenhagen, 89
Corness, Sydney, 55–7
Cottesmore, RAF [airfield], 14, 16
Couvron [airfield], 114
Cranfield, RAF [airfield], 16, 20–1
Creil, 51
Crisham, W/C Wiliam, 50
Cushing, Tommy, 177–8

Dakota, C47 [aircraft], 167
Darwin, RAAF [airfield], 155,
    157, 167
Dedelsdorf [airfield], 78, 82
Deelan [airfield], 53
Defiant [aircraft], 65
Dent, Ian, 179
DFC [award], 39, 53–4, 165, 183
Dinard-Pleurtuit [airfield], 46–7
Do 215 [aircraft], 49
Do 217 [aircraft], 55, 78, 86
Dorchester [hotel], 103
Douai [airfield], 33
DSO [award], 63, 101–102, 165
Dunn, Gp Cpt Wilfred, 21
Dunner-Zee [airfield], 93

East Wretham, RAF [airfield], 111
Edward [HM King], 8
Eindhoven, 86
Elmdon, RAF [airfield], 117
Emery, Gerald, 20
Enschede, 59
Everard, Sir, 92

Evreux [airfield], 49, 57, 98, 103, 105
Exeter, RAF [airfield], 57

Fairey Battle [aircraft], 14, 20
Field, John, 155
Fielder, Isabel, 1
Fletcher, Walter, 30, 32, 35–6
Flower, [Operation], 93
Focke-Wulf 200 Condor [aircraft], 34
Ford, RAF [airfield], 29, 32, 34, 36, 38–9, 42, 46, 50, 52, 55–9, 81, 135
Foulsham, RAF [airfield], 111, 142
Frenzel, Hermann, 57
Freya [Radar}, 182
Fw 190 [aircraft], 217, 219

Garbutt, RAF [airfield], 157–8, 167
Goldie, Hector, 65
Goulding, Leonard, 114
Gilze-Rijen [airfield], 86
Gravesend, RAF [airfield], 135
Great Massingham, RAF [airfield], 112
Gregory, Albert, 46
Gregory, Bill, 114, 119, 123
Grove [airfield], 182

Haamstede, 60
Halifax [aircraft], 179
Hannover, 77
Harris, Alf, 67
Harrow [School], 2
Hart [aircraft], 8
Havoc [aircraft], 29, 34–5, 38–9, 42–3, 53–4

He 111 [aircraft], 31, 36, 42
He 219 [aircraft], 223
Heath, Thomas, 78, 83
Henlow, RAF [airfield], 23, 25, 54
Hesepe [airfield], 93
Heycock, W/C George, 39, 170
High Ercall, RAF [airfield], 65–8, 70
Hill, AM Sir Roderic Maxwell, 85, 91
Hillingdon House, 43
Hoare, Cyril, 1
Hoare, Lucy, 142–8, 152, 156, 159, 172
Hoare, Hermione, 1, 169
Hodgson, Thomas, 125
Hunsdon, RAF [airfield], 60

Johns, Frederick, 115
Ju 88 [aircraft], 34–6, 207
Ju 188 [aircraft], 90, 222
Jutland, 123
Juvincourt [airfield], 51, 53

Kirton-in-Lindsay, RAF [airfield], 50
Krause, Johannes, 211

Lambert, W/C Frederick, 167
Laon [airfield], 114
Laupheim [airfield], 80
Le Bourget [airfield], 34, 36
Le Culot [airfield], 81, 95
Leconfield, RAF [airfield], 65
Leeuwarden [airfield], 98
Lee Mallory, ACM Sir Trafford, 83
Leigh, W/C Rupert, 43, 198

Leigh Mallory, ACM
    Sir Trafford, 83
Liberator [aircraft], 167
Lille Nord [airfield], 30
Little Snoring, RAF [airfield],
    110–12, 116, 119, 122, 128, 136,
    140, 142, 167, 180, 183, 186
London Gazette [Newspaper], 8,
    14, 29, 39, 43, 53, 56, 63, 93,
    101, 117, 130, 148
Longford, Frank, 160
Lorenz [locator], 56, 59, 90, 203–204
Luftwaffe, 9
Lugge, Con Thomas, 163, 168
Lysander [aircraft], 128

Macdonald, AC, 105
Maisch [airfield], 124
Manston [airfield], 30, 32–3, 46,
    75, 103
Maxwell, W/C Gerald, 135
McCarthy, Rev James, 161, 163
McEwen, John, 83
Me 109 [aircraft], 100, 217, 219
Me 262 [aircraft], 217–18, 223
Melun [airfield], 42
MID [award], 93, 103, 135, 148, 165
Middle Wallop [airfield], 39
Montdidier [airfield], 49
Moore, Robert, 117, 119
Morley, Henry, 117
Morris, Peter, 30–1, 169
Mosquito [aircraft], 54–60, 75, 77,
    80–3, 89–90, 93, 95, 97, 103,
    112, 114–15, 123, 125, 128,
    134–6, 152, 155, 157–8, 160,
    162, 167, 179–80, 207, 210

Muir, Robert, 83, 89–90, 93, 95,
    97–8, 100, 103, 135–6
Mulcair, Kevin, 86, 92
Murphy, W/C Alan, 125, 128–, 170,
    181, 186

Northolt, RAF [airfield], 9
Nordhorn [airfield], 93
Norton, Douglas, 77–8
Nuffield, Lord, 24

Order of Patriotic War [award], 89
Orleans-Bricy [airfield], 56
Overlord [Operation), 123

Packer, Frank, 173
Paris, 34, 36, 42, 56, 84
Pattinson, AM Sir Lawrence, 26, 64
Pegram, Ronald, 51
Pershore, RAF [airfield], 152
Porte, GC, 137
Potter, John, 55, 60, 77–8, 84–6
Potter, John, 55, 59–60, 77–8,
    80–1, 84–6

Rabone, Paul, 115, 117
RCAF, 46, 83, 86
Redwood, John, 134
Reid, Robert, 129
Renaut, W/C Michael, 179
Richards, Owain, 78
RNZAF, 152, 155
Rupprecht, Hans, 78
Russell, W/C Phil, 140

Salusbury-Hughes. F/L Kenderick, 47
Salzburg, 135

Salzwedel, 101
Saunders, ACM Arthur, 148
Scampton, RAF [airfield], 14
Schiphol, 92
Schunaufer, Heinz, 206, 210, 212
Sherrington, Roy, 32, 36, 170
Shipley, Edwin, 10
Singapore, 148, 150, 155, 173
Skinderholm 9airfield0, 123
Slee, GC Leonard, 110
Smith, John, 119
Soesterberg, 97
South Eastern Agricultural
    [School], 3
St Léger [airfield], 33
Starr, W/C Norman, 103
Stend, 100
Stendel, 95
Stenuit, Robert, 82
Stewart, George, 122, 183
Stokes, Daphne, 66–7, 70
Stokes, Peter, 66, 70
Stuggart, 98
Sunds [airfield], 123
Sutton, F/L Ken, 46
Sydney Island, 161–4

Tadzee [dog], 34
Tangmere, RAF [airfield], 46
Temperley, Nicholas, 20
Tergnier [airfield], 53
Thwaite, Thomas, 165
Thomas, William, 39
Tippell, Edwin, 157
Tomalin, W/C Charles, 75
Townsend, W/C Bill, 158, 167

Townsend, Gp Cpt Peter, 43
Trenchard, MRAF Lord, 76
Trenchard, Lord Marshall RAF, 76
Tutor [aircraft], 8
Twente, 59–60
Twinwood, RAF [airfield], 65, 74

Upavon, RAF [airfield], 119
USAAF, 152
Uxbridge, RAF [airfield], 13, 43

Vechta, 78, 93
VHF [radio], 57, 156, 158,
    215, 222
Villacoublay [airfield], 37–8
Vornhusen, Franz, 78–9

Wardell, Richard, 21
Wellesley [aircraft], 14
Wesendorf [airfield], 136
West Raynham, RAF
    [airfield], 110
Willoughby de Broke, GC Lord, 76,
    91, 105
Wilkinson, Norman, 81
Winkeligh, RAF airfield
    [airfield], 119
Wittering, RAF [airfield], 8–9
Woodbridge, RAF [airfield], 100,
    182–3
Worthy Down, RAF [airfield], 14
Wright, AC John, 105
Wunstorf [airfield], 93
Wykeham-Barnes, W/C Peter, 63

Zwolle, 128–9